YOU GOT THIS.

IVAN JOSEPH

YOU

Mastering the Skill of Self-Confidence

GOT THIS.

CALYPSO GROVE
PRESS

Calypso Groves Press
Toronto ON

Cataloguing data available from Library and Archives Canada
ISBN 978-0-9958300-0-4 (print)
ISBN 978-0-9958300-1-1 (ebook)

Produced by Page Two
www.pagetwostrategies.com
Copy editor: Lindsay Humphreys
Cover and interior design by Peter Cocking

17 18 19 20 21 5 4 3 2 1

To each and every one of you who has felt the pain of defeat and the paralysis of failure: believe in yourself and find that one person who believes in you no matter what.

This book is dedicated to my rock: Polly Joseph.

CONTENTS

1

BECOME A CRAZY ONE

THE SKILL OF SELF-CONFIDENCE

"If I keep on saying to myself that I cannot do a certain thing, it is possible that I may end by really becoming incapable of doing it. On the contrary, if I have the belief that I can do it, I shall surely acquire the capacity to do it even if I may not have it at the beginning."

MAHATMA GANDHI

ONE SUNDAY NIGHT in 2014, I sat looking out over the Dallas skyline from the window of a fancy room that had been provided for me at the Hilton Anatole. It was late and I needed to be up early to deliver the keynote address at the general session of the Women's Foodservice Forum (WFF) Annual Leadership Development Conference. There would be three thousand people in the room—far and away the largest group I had ever spoken to—all seeking guidance for their personal leadership journey. My topic, the skill of self-confidence, was familiar to me. I had delivered it dozens of times, mostly to students and small groups of leaders. And though my 2012 TEDx Talk, much to my surprise, now has over 8 million views, the idea of speaking to three thousand professionals had me quivering, thinking to myself, *I'm going to do* this? *Are you kidding me?!* Speaking to a group in return for a T-shirt, coffee mug, bottle of wine or warm pat on the back is easy—you just go up there and do it, no pressure. But the WFF folks were serious about achieving success and were paying me a lot of money to speak. For goodness' sake, Maya Angelou was one of the other speakers! I was way out of my league.

Since I had arrived at the conference, the organizers had treated me like royalty. I'd attended their opening-night event, which included the presentation of the Trailblazer Award to one of the prominent leaders in their community. I had toured the space where I would be speaking. I had walked around the opulent hotel and taken in the stunning lights, pools and spaces. And now I was sitting in this huge room with my head spinning, ready to curl up and die. Self-doubt had taken over. Forget about being an expert in self-confidence: I felt lower than a snake's belly in a wagon rut. I sat there looking out over the city and asking, "What am *I* doing here?" Note the emphasis on the "I."

Part of my struggle that night had to do with my history. I came to Canada from Guyana at age five when my older sister, Pam, and I flew to Toronto with nothing but the clothes we were wearing. There, we met our parents, who had left home five years before, two weeks after my birth. They were part of the "bright flight"—an exodus of educated Guyanese who were fleeing from the Communist regime and seeking a better life in England and North America. Back home, my father had been a sugar plantation manager, but when he completed a bachelor of science degree at McGill University in Montreal, there was no job to be found in his field and no prospect of returning to Guyana. So when Pam and I joined

NO ONE
WILL
BELIEVE
IN YOU
UNLESS
YOU DO.

our parents, we lived at Jane and Finch, one of the poorest neighborhoods in Toronto, known equally for its honest, hardworking, low-income population and for the highest concentration of criminal gangs in the country. We were as poor as potatoes; my father sold encyclopedias door-to-door at night to get by. He also got up at 4 a.m. every day to hitch-hike north to a dairy farm outside the city limits, where he worked as a laborer. In time, we moved closer to that farm once we could afford a small apartment. And then eventually the farm owner, Lorne Goodwill (his actual name!), offered us a small house on his property and even provided us with some furnishings and clothing. When I was old enough, I worked the farm side by side with Lorne's son, Robert, who was the same age and like a brother to me. It was the classic immigrant upbringing where nothing is taken for granted. It was also a life filled with the love of family and the certainty that only hard work will get you where you want to go.

Sitting in that elegant hotel magnified my sensation that I was out of place. What did I have to offer a room full of successful business leaders? So I tried to focus on how I ended up in that room. Random images came to mind. Moments in my life when I had faced adversity or started something new. Times when I had overcome an obstacle even though it seemed unlikely or even impossible that I could succeed. Thinking about it, I came up with a pretty long list.

First, I thought about my experiences at Joseph A. Gibson Public School, north of Toronto. I stood out like a raisin in a sugar bowl there—my sister Pam and I were two of only four black kids in the entire school. Color stopped at Steeles Avenue in those days because public transit only ran that far north. I used to get in fights when local kids picked on me for my Guyanese accent because I had not yet learned to speak "Canadian."

Then I remembered the weekend Robert and I were put in charge of the entire dairy farm at age 11. We ran ourselves ragged, alternately panicking and laughing hysterically as we milked and mucked and oversaw the entire operation.

I remembered growing up playing rep soccer with kids three years older than me. Pam played with the boys because there were no girls' teams and my dad only had time to coach one team—so I had to play up every year. I remembered attending Bayview Secondary School and being so poor that my track coach gave me a gym bag so I wouldn't have to carry my clothes and shoes around in a plastic grocery bag.

Then I thought about my university education. When I was in my senior year of high school, a recruiter from Graceland University in Iowa offered me a dual track and soccer scholarship. At the time, I thought going to school in Iowa would be like an episode of *Green Acres*, so I turned it down, opting instead to attend Laurentian University in Ontario. I had been a gym rat throughout high school and Laurentian had a renowned sport management and kinesiology program. When I got there, I fell in the trap that so many first-year students face—I lost my sense of purpose and starting living the country club life. I missed classes; I socialized;

"I have come to the frightening conclusion that I am the decisive element. It is my personal approach that creates the climate. It is my daily mood that makes the weather."

HAIM G. GINOTT

Teacher and Child: A Book for Parents and Teachers

I had fun. And long before I realized what was going on, my lifestyle caught up with me. I failed some courses, misunderstood the guidelines for probation and was, eventually, kicked out. Only when I was working at Foot Locker and McDonald's did the reality of what had happened sink in. I hated feeling stupid. (The failure was so humiliating that I didn't tell my parents about it until I was 39!) Eventually my determination to change kicked in and I contacted Brian Shantz, the recruiter who had offered me the scholarship at Graceland, to see if I could get a second chance. Thankfully, Brian made it happen and I went to Graceland to start over—as a black student-athlete in an almost entirely white town consisting of a mere thousand people in the middle of the corn desert. (Talk about living in the sugar bowl!) Having learned my lesson, when I got there I focused on my courses and logged immeasurable hours in the library. I got top grades. I went on to become Student Body President. I played soccer and ran track. I turned my life around.

That night in the hotel, I also remembered the stages of my career. At first, I was balancing the demands of coaching men's soccer and being a residence director of Gunsolley Hall at Graceland with studying for a master's degree at Drake University. Then I added being an assistant professor to the list and enrolled in a PhD program, while coaching the soccer team to the national championship. My wife Polly and I also started a family, owned 10 houses that we fixed up and rented out, and operated a Laundromat. Later, when we left Iowa, I accepted a position at Ryerson

University—a huge urban university in Toronto—taking over an athletic program that had been the laughingstock of the country for decades. When I was hired, the president was very clear: he wanted teams that could unite the campus by competing for the national championship every year. Oh, and he wanted me to oversee the $100-million renovation of Maple Leaf Gardens (Canada's onetime version of Madison Square Garden or Fenway Park), which had been acquired by Ryerson.

Over and over again, I had been in situations that stretched me beyond what I had already done. Sometimes it just happened; other times it was something I pursued. Either way, each and every time I felt the same crushing self-doubt that was pressing down on me that Dallas night. I mean, seriously... what was a kid who could barely afford his lunch now doing in a marble-clad hotel room preparing to speak at a massive corporate gathering? As it turned out, I was doing what I always did: believing I could translate honed skills into a new situation.

Having studied, taught, trained and spoken about excelling under pressure for so many years, I knew how to sit with the fear and channel that anxiousness toward my performance. This doesn't mean I was able to calm down; in fact, I was shaking like a rattler's tail when I woke up the next morning. It just means that I knew how to make the pressure work for me. For example, I was breathing so hard when I finally arrived on stage that I had to make a joke about the stairs giving me quite a workout. And then I started the presentation with an audience visualization exercise that we use in sports psychology. I told the crowd it was intended to get them in the mood—which it was—but it also gave me a chance to catch my breath and get into the groove.

In the end, the speech went well, not because I had practiced it so many times, but because I had been in enough situations to develop my belief in me. Long before I even knew what self-confidence was, I was building it. So by the time I got up there on stage, it wasn't novel for me to respond to fear and self-doubt with an ability to perform. As stressful as the night and morning had been, I knew I could do it because I had come through similar situations so many times before.

The Skill of Self-Confidence

"You gain strength, courage and confidence by every experience in which you really stop to look fear in the face... You must do the thing you think you cannot do."
ELEANOR ROOSEVELT

The year I took over as head coach of the men's soccer team at Graceland, we had a problem. The team had performed decently in the local conference, but it had never done much beyond that. Right away, I focused on a goal that seemed impossible in a school of only 1,000 students: win a national championship. To do that, we needed to think about performance in a whole new way. So I enrolled in a

PhD program in sports psychology and began to explore the mental side of sport.

The overlap between my studies and coaching meant I could use the players like a living laboratory. Together, we explored new theories to see if they worked. We had a ton of fun trying out the ideas, but it was nothing compared to the change in performance that followed. My players started to succeed like never before—individually and as a team. Within four years, the team went from being number one or two in the local conference to being nationally ranked. First they were twenty-third, then tenth, then first, and eventually they won the national championship, an accomplishment so beyond the scope of imagination that the entire town attended the celebration parade.

Looking back on the team's success, I know there were technical elements that made it possible for our little school to win: practice drills, strategy, and even the way we watered, cut and sodded our field. But the mental development of the players was the game changer. Shifting the way they thought about themselves allowed them to handle the pressures and work together like never before.

What I learned during those years has been the basis of my career ever since: great performance requires mental qualities such as being able to focus, recover from setbacks and work cohesively with peers. Teach athletes the right mental skills, and they'll acquire what they need more than anything: self-confidence. Confident athletes are successful in the same ways that confident people are successful: They

SELF-CONFIDENT PEOPLE BELIEVE IN THEMSELVES

WHEN OTHERS DO NOT.

handle pressure better. They channel anxiety into improved performances. They want to be at the center of the action, and they rise to the occasion whenever they are.

I think of self-confidence as *the belief in your ability to accomplish the task at hand.* That doesn't mean being deluded that you can do impossible things, like in that commercial where the flight attendant informs the passengers that the captain has had a heart attack, and you put up your hand and say, "I can do it. I just stayed at a Holiday Inn Express!" Self-confidence is a belief that you can do something beyond your current level of experience and skill. It's also having faith that you can handle adversity, and even if it doesn't turn out exactly as you had hoped, you know you did your best.

Dozens of studies have been conducted about the role that confidence plays in our ability to turn thoughts into action. For example, renowned psychologist Albert Bandura discovered that confident people see difficult tasks as challenges to be overcome rather than situations to avoid. He also found that confident people recover more quickly from setbacks and respond with increased effort, both of which are critical for long-term success.

Another advantage of believing in yourself is that it can lead to a better quality of life. Research shows that confidence is related to better mental and physical health, higher educational achievement, improved literacy, lower dropout rates and better economic standing. You don't need to be a Harvard grad to have self-confidence, but if you have self-confidence you are more likely to attend a better school, get a better job and lead a better life. In fact, there is significant evidence that self-confidence is a more important factor in determining success than talent is!

Confident people aren't any taller, smarter, better-looking or richer than you or me, and an Ivy League education isn't required. What they have is a belief in themselves, which anyone can develop. The difficulty is that most people view self-confidence as an inborn quality that someone either has or doesn't have. I have met so many folks who think, *I'm just not the kind of person who is confident about their abilities.* Maybe you are one of those people. Maybe you figure you were out picking up bread when they passed out the confidence gene, that you don't have it and you can't get it. Nothing could be further from the truth. Self-confidence is a global skill that anyone—and I mean *anyone*—can learn.

Putting yourself in situations where you overcome challenges or obstacles—over and over again, even if they are relatively small—develops the skill of self-confidence. You don't need to win a national championship or oversee a $100-million athletic facility. You just need to do something that challenges you. Maybe it's volunteering as an assistant so you can learn from the best, getting back into the job market after you have been fired or sending your manuscript in again after ten rejections and having it be accepted. With each small increase in challenge you take on, you gain a bit more belief in your ability to succeed until you are so confident that success is no more difficult than getting to work on time or calling a friend.

"Promise me you'll always remember: You're braver than you believe, and stronger than you seem, and smarter than you think."

CHRISTOPHER ROBIN
TO WINNIE THE POOH

➤ WRITING PROMPT

List three small challenges you will take on to begin your journey toward a more self-confident you:

1 ______________________________

2 ______________________________

3 ______________________________

The Crazy Ones

"If one advances confidently in the direction of his dreams, and endeavors to live the life which he has imagined, he will meet with a success unexpected in common hours."
HENRY DAVID THOREAU

At the beginning of every soccer season or any speech I give about self-confidence, I show the "Crazy Ones" commercial from Apple's 1997 Think Different campaign—the one with famous innovators like Pablo Picasso, Martin Luther King Jr., John Lennon, Amelia Earhart, Jim Henson and Albert Einstein. If you've never seen it, you should search for it right now and take it in. (In the version that went on the air, the voiceover was done by Richard Dreyfuss, but there is also a version with Steve Jobs himself narrating.)

I will never forget how it made me feel when I saw that ad for the first time. My spine tingled from the instant I heard those first words: "Here's to the crazy ones. The misfits. The rebels. The troublemakers." And since then, every time I see the video my heart races all the way to that incredible final line: "The people who are crazy enough to think they can change the world are the ones who do."

If we want to, any of us can become a crazy one. Sure, we may not lead a civil rights movement or fly a plane across the Atlantic or invent a device that revolutionizes the world, but we never know what we can accomplish. We are all engaged in things that matter. We are all living our *one life*. And we all have an opportunity, every single day, to do it better. To be a better parent, friend, spouse or coworker. To help someone out. To invent a new way. To make a bold suggestion. To speak out against injustice. To create something original. You never know what you can accomplish until you try.

➤ WRITING PROMPT

Bring your crazy idea out into the daylight—write it here (this requires bravery on your part):

___

___

___

It's an illusion to think that greatness belongs to a privileged few who act on the global stage. Every one of us has the capacity to be great. I have seen this truth play out over and over again in my own life—in my research, in my coaching career and in my experiences speaking all over North America. Every life is wonderful and worthwhile. Yours matters. You are not small because you won't change history. What matters is whatever you care about. *Your life.* Sure, the pressures you face in a cubicle or gym or corner office may not be the same as those faced by the starting quarterback in the Super Bowl, but they are no less *important*. They matter to you as much as anything matters to anyone. And all you need to do to achieve your best life is to believe in yourself.

FAMOUS FAILURE

In 1919, Walt Disney was fired from his job at the *Kansas City Star* newspaper because his editor thought he "lacked imagination and had no good ideas."

Mine is a story of self-confidence. Yours will be too. You can use this book as a practical guide to develop the skill of self-confidence and put that skill to use in your day-to-day life. At work, at home, at school and in everything you do, you can become a high-performing individual—a better version of yourself.

With the skill of self-confidence, the sky is the limit.

2

REPETITION, REPETITION, REPETITION

HOW TO ACQUIRE A SKILL

"We are what we repeatedly do."

ARISTOTLE

I'M OLD ENOUGH that I learned how to drive on a stick shift. Initially, it takes everything you have to get the car moving without stalling or burning out the clutch. You're concentrating like mad, and after that first 10-minute lesson you need a nap. But the next time, you get off the curb with relative ease and head down the street feeling like a pro, thinking *I got this!* Then you come to a stop sign and a car pulls up behind you and suddenly you are filled with the fear of God. But you get through—with or without stalling and having to put on your hazard lights as you restart. And then, in time, you get pretty good at stopping and starting, so you get sassy and decide to drive downtown. This time, you end up stopped on a hill with a dump truck behind you. Bloody hell! Now you're sweating buckets and freaking out and trying to focus on what your hands and feet are doing. Are you giving it enough gas? Have you released the clutch enough? And the whole time you are praying, *Dear*

God, please let me get this right! It takes all you have to get through it and you need a week to recover. But you do it.

Now fast-forward 1,000 miles and you're not even thinking about driving. You're talking on the phone (hands-free, of course), singing along with the radio and snacking on mango chips. Driving stick is easy! Well, driving stick is the same as it was before; it just became automatic for you. Through practice and repetition, you took it from an overwhelming, foreign and novel skill to something you do automatically. The skill became a habit. Building a belief in your ability to accomplish a task at hand—becoming self-confident—is no different. It's just a skill you need to acquire.

How Can a Mental Attribute Be a Skill?

When I suggest to people that self-confidence is a skill, I get a lot of raised eyebrows and frowns in response. *Sure*, they think. *Shooting a soccer ball is a skill you can practice. But your belief in yourself isn't like that.* Except it is. Humans are highly adept at developing new ways of thinking because our brains are *plastic*. Not the hard stuff your laundry detergent comes in, but flexible stuff that can change and grow depending on how you use it. No matter how old you are, your brain continues to change shape in response to your thinking, your habits and your experiences.

One famous study that reveals how plastic our brains are was conducted on taxi drivers in one of the most complex and intricate cities in the world: London, England. Cabbies there have to undergo extensive training for two years to attain what locals call "being on The Knowledge." This phrase means having enough information in your head to manage getting to the thousands of locations around the city.

Researchers put London taxi drivers in a structural MRI machine and scanned their brains—specifically the hippocampus, which is where we store spatial information for navigation. When compared with a control group of non-taxi drivers, the taxi drivers' brains had much larger spatial centers. Why? Because they essentially have to hold a map of London in their minds to navigate. Every day, every shift, every fare, they build a neural network, and as a result specific areas of their brains grow larger!

How your brain grows depends on the demands you make of it. If you do something over and over again, your brain will change size and shape to meet the needs of that task. So if you repeat any mental activity over time, like learning how to drive a stick shift, your brain will bulk up until one day that skill feels effortless. The takeaway here is that repeating particular thoughts and habits changes your brain, just like it does for London cabbies. That's how you build self-confidence: you use your brain differently, it changes as a result, and you gain a mental skill you didn't have before.

Mental skills are actually easier to acquire than physical ones. To dunk a basketball, you need height and light, springy, strong muscles. To run 100 meters in under 10 seconds, you need particular kinds of type II muscles and platinum wiring in your nervous system. And having seen more than my fair share of aspiring soccer players with goat hooves for feet, I can tell you that you have to have something special to dribble or trap a ball while running, spinning and jumping. But it's different with mental skills, especially universal qualities like self-confidence. You don't need to have extraordinary physical gifts. You just need to have the basic mental and emotional makeup that we all share.

To build mental skills, you approach your "training" in the same way an athlete does to develop strength, endurance and sport-specific abilities. You can follow a simple three-part model, outlined below, that great coaches have been using for years to help athletes develop.

Skill Builder #1: Repeat to Acquire

In order to acquire a skill, you have to repeat it over and over again. Coaches call this "blocked practice." Doing the same activity again and again forges neural connections between your muscles and your mind that grow into habits. That's why athletes all the way up to the elite level spend time practicing basic skills, like shooting and passing.

My most powerful memory of blocked practice involves Carlos Ortiz, a six-foot-four goalkeeper from Colombia who played for me at Graceland. When Carlos first joined the team, his hands were made of stone and he had real difficulty throwing the ball accurately. So we set him up in front of a

REPETITION

RE**PE**TITION

REPE**TI**TION

REPETI**TION**

REPETI**TION**

REPE**TI**TION

RE**PE**TITION

REPETITION

"Most people live in a very restricted circle of their potential being. They make use of a very small portion of their possible consciousness, and of their soul's resources in general, much like a man who, out of his whole organism, should get into a habit of using and moving only his little finger."

WILLIAM JAMES

brick wall and drew a chalk line around one of the bricks. His job was to hit the same spot over and over again. He went at the task like a man possessed, throwing the ball thousands of times until his hands were calloused and hard. And it worked. He trained himself to throw the ball exactly where he wanted to without even thinking about it. And he built skills so strong that he went on to play professional soccer with a variety of international teams. Then he came back to the game as a coach, first at Graceland and now at Seton Hall University.

Your mental and emotional equivalent of what Carlos achieved physically requires putting yourself in situations that use the same mental skill over and over again. Need to work on how you handle setbacks? Go fail at something. Need to get better at paying attention? Find something to concentrate on. It's that simple. By repeating the particular skill, you will acquire it. Repetition, repetition, repetition.

Skill Builder #2: Vary to Retain

Repetition is the key to acquiring a skill in the first place, but it's not the key to retaining it for the long term. To do this, you need to use a version of what coaches call "random practice" (also known as variable practice), which means performing the skill in bursts intermixed with sessions of other skills. For example, say I had two groups of soccer players. One group does nothing but work on throw-ins while the other group works on throw-ins, free kicks and headers. By the end of the session, the throw-in specialists will have advanced that particular skill much further than the generalists. But if I bring them back in a week, the athletes who spread their focus between three different activities will have *retained* the new skills more than the specialist group will have.

This is the result of what's called "spaced repetition." Your brain is far more likely to transfer learning from short-term memory to long-term memory if you practice something in small chunks spread out over time. Practicing the piano for an hour a day over the course of a week will advance your skills more than practicing for seven hours once per week will. It's the difference between the learning you didn't really do while cramming for an exam in high school and the learning you actually do at work through daily repetition.

So, along with practicing your mental skill, it's best to mix it up so that you work on a skill for a bit, leave it alone while you do other things, and then come back to it. Actually, this part is easy because your normal routines of living and working will probably provide you with all the variety you need to ensure your skill retention. Just remember the key concept: to improve and retain a skill, one hour a day for a week is better than seven hours a day once a week.

Skill Builder #3: Take Small Steps

One of the biggest challenges for a coach is knowing exactly what the players need every single day. If you don't challenge them enough, they get bored, stop performing well and begin to dislike practices. If you challenge them too much, they get overwhelmed, feel like they are no good and want to quit. Every time I arrived at practice, I had to figure out exactly how much my players could handle on that particular day—as a team and individually. I also had to make sure that I followed the most important rule of skill development: only add one new stimulus at a time. It was important that the players had mastered the last skill before I added a new one. If I did it right, their sense at every stage was that learning the new skill was easy—even if it was significantly advanced from where they were a few weeks before.

FAMOUS FAILURE

Thomas Edison's teachers said he was "too stupid to learn anything," and he was fired from his first two jobs for being "non-productive."

For example, if I were trying to teach a new defensive system, I would start out with a one-on-one drill so that the players could learn the new skill while only defending against one attacker. Then, once they all had the skill, I would add a second defender and make it a one-on-two. Then, over the course of a few weeks, I would keep adding bodies to the drills—one-on-three, two-on-three, three-on-four, five-on-seven, and so on—until I got to an 11-on-11 situation where we could simulate game conditions. By approaching it this way, I could teach a complex system in a simple way. And the players never got overwhelmed, angry or tense. They just came to practice and enjoyed the wonderful sensation of improving.

In a work setting the same approach could apply, for example, to a person developing their presentation skills over an extended period of time. Initially, they might speak in a department meeting or give their direct supervisor a briefing on a project. Then they could deliver a project update to a group of department heads. After that, they might present to the management team on their way to facing an entire division. The same kind of graduated presentation process can be used when learning how to present to customers. You could start with speaking to an individual client and slowly add complexity and pressure until you're ready to make the big pitch to the decision-makers at a large corporation. Small steps lead to big growth.

This last element of the three-step model is the most important if you want to succeed. If you try to learn too many new skills at once, you will feel overwhelmed and be hugely disappointed when you aren't up to the task. Or if you limit your focus to only one skill but try to reach way too far, you'll flop and take a while to recover. Look for experiences that push you just the right amount until you master the skill. Then you can move on to the next challenge. That way, you will maintain your motivation over the long term and achieve substantial success. Real progress requires slow and steady development because you can't change your brain overnight. And if you aren't engaged and happy along the way, you'll quit and fall back into your old habits. Start simple, take small steps one at a time and work your way toward mastering complex skills until you achieve the emotional equivalent of an Olympic gold medal in confidence.

MANY OF US WILL REPEAT SOME-THING, BUT HOW MANY OF US WILL PERSIST?

THE SECRET IS REPETITION WITH PERSISTENCE

THE SECRET IS REPETITION WITH PERSISTENCE.

➤ WRITING PROMPT

Commit to building your skill. Set aside seven minutes a day. Put it in ink here:

Monday	:	a.m./p.m.
Tuesday	:	a.m./p.m.
Wednesday	:	a.m./p.m.
Thursday	:	a.m./p.m.
Friday	:	a.m./p.m.
Saturday	:	a.m./p.m.
Sunday	:	a.m./p.m.

Remember, the journey of self-confidence begins with a single step.

The Five Mental Skills

While self-confidence is a master skill you can develop, it's important to understand that it is not a single quality that stands alone at the heart of a successful person. Instead,

NO MATTER HOW OLD YOU ARE, YOUR BRAIN CONTINUES TO CHANGE IN RESPONSE TO YOUR THINKING, HABITS AND EXPERIENCES.

self-confidence happens when several different mental skills combine. In my experience, I have learned that there are five supporting mental skills: positive thought, team building, grit, higher expectations and focus. In the chapters that follow, I address each of these mental skills individually, but I believe it is their constellation that leads to the master skill of self-confidence, not any one of them operating alone. Like the muscles of a body, the parts of the brain, the members of an orchestra, the staff of an organization or, as has been the case in my career, the players on a team, the five skills are a group working together to create confidence and drive achievement. With unity among these skills—when they are all doing their part to enrich our lives and our work—we will have acquired a deep belief in our ability to accomplish the task at hand. With that belief and capacity to succeed, we can uncover our purpose in life and get on with achieving our dreams.

CHAPTER 2 RECAP

How to Acquire a Skill

Skill Builder #1: Repeat to Acquire

Perform a mental skill over and over again until you can do it without thinking.

Skill Builder #2: Vary to Retain

Intersperse working on a particular skill with working on other skills to ensure long-term retention.

Skill Builder #3: Take Small Steps

Ensure that you have fully mastered your current level of a given skill before adding a more difficult challenge—and when you do so, only increase the challenge by a reasonable amount so that success is possible.

3

THINK YOU CAN

THE SKILL OF POSITIVE THOUGHT

"I am the greatest."

MUHAMMAD ALI

WHEN I ARRIVED at Graceland University, I was so grateful for the opportunity—and so disappointed about my previous flop at Laurentian University—that I passed up on popularity and fun to prove I could excel academically. Whenever I wasn't at track or soccer practice, I was in my room or the library studying. Basically, I was a hermit. It was a very strange year for me, but it led to two wonderful things. First, I achieved a 4.0 GPA. Second, in spring of that year, I met Polly—my life partner and soul mate. We were married while we were still students, and she has been my number-one supporter, critic and friend ever since.

At the conclusion of that year of endless studying, I was itching to get back to my number-one passion: sport. So in the summer before my sophomore year, I trained like crazy. I wanted a starting spot on the soccer team. I worked hard in tryouts and when they were over, I was chosen as one of the starting 11. I had achieved my goal, and I was ready to show my coach and teammates just how much of an impact I could have on the team. But that isn't what happened.

A few games into the season, we played a team from Columbia, Missouri, that was fifth in the nation, well above our team in the rankings. I went into the game intent on making a big splash and being the one who would carry us to new heights. And, like many young athletes whose egos get in the way of team play and consistent performance, my desire to be "the man" backfired. Fifteen minutes into the game, an opposing player broke free and headed toward our goal with the ball. I went to tackle him from behind and ended up pulling him down by his shirt, which is not allowed in soccer. The ref made the right call and gave me a red card. I was ejected and our team had to play shorthanded for the rest of the game.

When we ended up losing 2–0, the coach held me responsible. And I don't blame him. What I did was stupid and selfish. So when he told me that I would be sitting out the next game, I wasn't really surprised. But I was surprised when I also sat out the second game; shocked when I sat out the third; furious when I sat out the fourth. As the suspension dragged on, I started to think about giving up soccer and, as a result, my effort started to dwindle. I could tell that the other players' attitude toward me was changing, and it seemed to me like the coach didn't care about me anymore. My own attitude was also changing. I was having the typical reaction of an athlete who feels embarrassed and hurt: I decided I didn't care.

CHANGE
YOUR
THOUGHTS

SO YOU CAN PERFORM AT YOUR BEST.

There was one moment during the suspension I will never forget. We were in the middle of a game, and I was sitting on the bench with the other substitutes when the coach suddenly called on me to go in for an injured starter. I was shocked. "Me?" I asked him, incredulous. "Yes," he replied. "*You.*" I stood up and automatically started to pull off my warm-up suit only to remember that I hadn't bothered to put on my uniform underneath! I had assumed I wouldn't see any playing time at all. The coach was furious and told me to go back to the bench where I belonged. You would have thought I'd be devastated. I wasn't. Truth is, I had decided not to wear my uniform because of the battle of wills I had entered into with the coach. I figured I would stick it to him instead of letting him stick it to me. So I sauntered back to the bench with every ounce of cool I could gather. But inside, I was sinking. That kind of behavior just isn't me. And so, as I sat there, I sank lower and lower.

FAMOUS FAILURE

Michael Jordan was cut from his high school varsity basketball team in his sophomore year.

When the game was over, I figured I had secured my future on the bench for a long time and was just about ready to quit for good. I walked over to the bleachers and sat down while my teammates, friends and all of the fans left the field. That's when Polly came over. We sat quietly for a while; me slumped over and embarrassed, her looking out over the field. When she finally spoke, it was in a way I had never heard from her before.

"I don't understand why you're letting this coach make you feel so bad about yourself if you are a great player," she said. "Weren't you one of the best in the province back home? And captain of your team? And isn't the level of soccer here not as good as it is there?" When I didn't object, she continued. "Then why are you acting like you don't belong? Why are you giving him so much power? Why are you letting him decide if you are good or not? You have to believe in yourself and just go out there and do your best—no matter what he decides to do. You have to show him you belong."

I listened quietly to what Polly was saying and then spent the night thinking about it. I knew she was right. And I began to see that I was letting my thoughts influence my actions and behaviors. I was letting external forces create negative thoughts about myself and my ability. I saw that giving up on soccer actually was giving up on me.

The next day, I woke up a changed man. *Polly is right! My attitude is the problem*, I remember thinking. *I need to take responsibility for myself and not blame the coach or give him a reason not to play me. I* am *a good soccer player. I* can *do it. I know I can be the best. I'm going to work so hard that he has no choice but to play me.* So I did. I went to practice and played like a man possessed. I did so well in practice that the coach had no choice but to start me in an upcoming game. And I was so focused in the rest of the games that I was chosen as an all-star at the end of the season and selected to be team captain the next year. In fact, after my playing days were over, I went on to become the assistant coach on the team

"Every thought we think is defining our future."

LOUISE HAY

and worked side by side with that coach. All because I had made a decision to change the way I *thought* about me and my performance.

My soccer experience was a lot like what happens when you don't get a promotion at work or when someone else takes the credit for something you did. If you let the situation dictate how you feel, you won't feel very good. But how you respond to any given situation is within your control. That day on the bleachers was the first time I realized how much influence our thoughts have on our performance. It was the beginning of my professional obsession with the idea that if we get our thinking right, we can do anything. This idea became the focus of my graduate studies and has fueled my entire coaching, administrative and speaking career. We are what we think we are. And just like in *The Little Engine That Could*, if you think you can, you will.

The Skill of Positive Thought

"The moment you doubt whether you can fly, you cease forever to be able to do it." J.M. BARRIE

We all have an audio track playing in our heads. A quiet little voice that repeats messages over and over again. And when that voice comes from the dark part of our heart, it is invariably negative. When I ask audience members at speaking engagements to share their negative thoughts, women tell me they think "My butt is too big" or "I'm not good enough to get ahead." Men say they think "My hairline is receding" or "I don't have enough money" or "My gut is too big" or "My car isn't cool enough." These thoughts are similar to ones we are all familiar with: "I'm stupid," "I can't do that," "This is too much for me," "I'm boring" and on and on. Negative thoughts plague us. And, more importantly, they are a significant problem for our performance.

Imagine someone whose opinion you value, like your boss or your spouse, saying you're not capable of doing something. Better yet, think about the effect of a parent's stream of negative talk that hammers away at their kid's belief in himself or herself. It's a constant assault. And that's exactly how the emotional core of our brain experiences it—as an assault. When someone hurls negative comments at us, we experience them as an attack that threatens our sense of self. Our stress response is triggered, our fight-or-flight mechanisms engage and our bodies fill with cortisol and adrenaline. Those chemicals are helpful in rare moments of actual crisis but damaging to our health in the face of life's typical stresses. Even athletes, who need to exert themselves at an intense physical level, falter if they experience performance pressure as a threat. They need to be energized, focused, even amped up—but in control. Fight or flight for an athlete means failure to perform. The same is true for all of us.

When negative comments come from inside our own minds, this "self-assault" triggers a stress response that hinders our problem-solving capacity and reduces our ability to perform. In a new or difficult situation, negative thoughts

"You are what you believe you are."

C.S. LEWIS

can grow so deafening that we become overwhelmed and slip into anxiousness: sweaty palms, high blood pressure and visions of worst-case scenarios.

So what can we do in tough situations, or when we're not certain or when we place too much pressure on ourselves? Learn to control our thoughts and create a positive outlook. If we can do this, we can capitalize on the enormous boost in performance that comes from having an optimistic mindset.

In his best-selling book *The Happiness Advantage*, Shawn Achor reports on a decade of research showing that happiness increases outcomes in a variety of sectors. People are

31 percent more productive when happy compared to when they are in a neutral, negative or stressed headspace. He found that those who are in sales are 37 percent more effective, and doctors are 19 percent faster and more accurate reaching a correct diagnosis.

The idea is simple: if we feel good, we perform well. And so by changing your thoughts, you change your game. There are several effective ways to improve your ability to think positively, which I'll look at now.

Positive Thought Builder #1: Stop Negative Thoughts

In sports psychology, the ability to shut out negative thoughts and replace them with the belief that you can succeed is called "thought stopping" or "centering." When you see a professional soccer player clap twice after they miss the net or point at an opposing player who just beat them, they are using a physical cue to snap out of self-doubt and be reminded that they are skilled and capable. It's the same process basketball and volleyball players use when they tap hands with each other on both good and bad shots. And why baseball pitchers take one deep breath as they mentally prepare for every pitch. These athletes have been trained to routinely replace thoughts about mistakes (either actual or possible) with messages about their ability, which they cue with physical actions.

When I coach soccer, I often give my athletes a rubber band and tell them to move the band from one wrist to another or give it a light snap whenever they have a negative thought. This develops an awareness of their thought tendencies so they can learn to shift to a positive outlook. The process becomes automatic and their performance improves. You can do this too. Decide on a simple physical gesture and repeat it every time an "I'm no good" or "I'm not up to the challenge" thought intrudes. You may, in fact, be in a tough situation at the time, but negative thoughts won't take you anywhere but down. Learn to recognize any mental habit that undermines your belief in yourself and take action to address it.

When I give speeches, I demonstrate the skill of thought stopping by asking for a volunteer from the audience. After the introductions and some light banter, I ask the person to close their eyes and think of a time when they were very successful. Then I ask them to hold one of their arms straight out to the side and try to resist me pushing down on their arm. We then repeat the exercise with them remembering a moment when they made a huge mistake. Every single time—I kid you not—when the person focuses on their failure, they are not able to hold up their arm as well. They are actually weaker. The exercise is not about strength; it's about thoughts influencing beliefs and actions. You can accept the negative thoughts and let them control you, or you can change your thoughts and perform at your best.

➤ WRITING PROMPT

What ritual will you use to interrupt your negative thoughts?

☐ Finger snap

☐ Ear rub

☐ Hand clap

☐ Other: ______

Positive Thought Builder #2: Use Affirmations

When he was imprisoned on Robben Island, Nelson Mandela's days involved a number of routines. There was the back-breaking labor he was forced to perform, of course, but some of Mandela's routines consisted of mental habits he formed in order to survive, two of which I find particularly interesting. One is that he told himself over and over again that the guards were human beings. He believed that if he saw them as people who had spouses and children and families, he could resist the hardening effects of his incarceration. He also believed that it would influence their behavior toward him. Mandela's other mental habit was to recite a poem he had memorized—one that is now well-known because its title was used by the Hollywood film starring Matt Damon and Morgan Freeman. The poem is called "Invictus" and was written by an otherwise unknown English poet named William Ernest Henley in 1875:

THREE

ONE

AFFIRMATIONS A

TWO

DAY INCREASES

THREE

YOUR PERFOR-

ONE

MANCE ON THE

TWO

JOB, AT HOME

THREE

AND IN LIFE.

Out of the night that covers me,
Black as the pit from pole to pole,
I thank whatever gods may be
For my unconquerable soul.

In the fell clutch of circumstance
I have not winced nor cried aloud.
Under the bludgeonings of chance
My head is bloody, but unbowed.

Beyond this place of wrath and tears
Looms but the Horror of the shade,
And yet the menace of the years
Finds and shall find me unafraid.

It matters not how strait the gate,
How charged with punishments the scroll,
I am the master of my fate,
I am the captain of my soul.

Whether Mandela knew it or not, these two mental habits were forms of daily affirmation. He repeated them to shape his thoughts in a positive direction and build his confidence. He put these mental skills to good use in a long struggle for freedom that, more than anything else, required an unwavering belief in his ability to accomplish the task at hand. He is one of the most powerful examples in history of how to change your position in life through having a positive mindset.

Simple affirmative phrases can change the negative thoughts that undermine your confidence. I have about 10 affirmations that I've developed over the years. I keep them on a written list posted at home and use them whenever I face something new, like when I spoke to that huge group in Texas or when I had to attend meetings with Toronto's business bigwigs to acquire the funds to buy and renovate Maple Leaf Gardens. I quietly say to myself, out loud, phrases such as "You got this, Ivan"; "Nobody outworks me"; "I choose to be happy." And my favorite, which was inspired by the poem: "I am captain of my ship. I am master of my fate." These statements help me reclaim my personal power so that I don't walk into a situation and allow someone else to determine how I feel or perform. They are also expressions of my belief in myself that calm me and help me channel my energy and anxiousness into my performance—just like elite athletes under immense pressure in the final play before time runs out.

Affirmations are more than a warm and fuzzy technique used by coaches (a lot of whom are not so warm and fuzzy!). They are a proven method of shaping and controlling our thoughts. Researchers at Carnegie Mellon University found that affirmations combat stress and can lead to positive effects in performance. The study showed that self-affirmation boosts the ability to solve problems under pressure and reduces the negative effects of chronic stress.

Another study published by the Association for Psychological Science indicates that self-affirmation enhances our performance by making us more aware of our errors and more emotionally comfortable with accepting and

"Change your thoughts and you change the world."

NORMAN VINCENT PEALE

correcting them. That's an interesting finding: Affirmations don't give us that false confidence where we deny we make mistakes at all and pass ourselves off as awesome or perfect. Instead, they make us strong enough to say, "Okay, I got that wrong, and now I'm going to fix it." That kind of thinking improves our performance.

I'll mention one more study, just in case you can't get past Al Franken's hilariously over-the-top version of a self-affirmation ("I'm good enough, I'm smart enough, and doggone it, people like me!") on *Saturday Night Live*. A Stanford University study revealed that affirmations enhance our belief in our personal power and make us less susceptible to threats from outside us. The research also confirmed that affirmations can improve education, health and relationships. All told, these are some impressive outcomes of the ability to shape our own thoughts.

An effective affirmation reminds you of your values and beliefs—of who you are. That is why I say, "You got this, Ivan." I am reminding myself of my belief that I can succeed even when nothing is handed to me. It's shorthand for "Ivan, you have what it takes to do this because you have done it before and you are the kind of person who will make it through the storm." Your affirmations are brief versions of deep beliefs about yourself. For example, Muhammad Ali's famous statement "I am the greatest" is shorthand for his belief in hard work and toughing it out against the odds. He has also put it this way: "Impossible is just a big word thrown around by small men who find it easier to live in the world they've been given than to explore the power they have to change it. Impossible is not a fact. It's an opinion. Impossible is not a declaration. It's a dare. Impossible is potential. Impossible is temporary. Impossible is nothing."

Develop affirmations for yourself. Focus on creating phrases that emphasize your best beliefs about yourself or your cherished values. These will remind you of what makes you unique, strong and capable. Use phrases like "I will never quit" or "I am strong" or "I have done it before and I will do it again," if those tap into your beliefs. And use them every day, especially in the morning and right before any task that makes you anxious or anticipate the worst. Just remember, it's not a magic button. You can't just start affirming yourself and hope that negative thoughts or stress will disappear. You have to repeat, repeat, repeat and ensure that the phrases are your *actual* beliefs and values, not things you wish you cared about. Repeat until you are so practiced at genuinely (not just wishfully) replacing fear and worry with belief in yourself that you don't even notice you are doing it. If you practice deliberately and often, you can rewire your brain until you think and feel different, simply because you made yourself do it.

DON'T ALLOW SOMEONE ELSE TO DETERMINE HOW YOU FEEL.

➤ WRITING PROMPT

List three positive affirmations about yourself:

I am ______________________________

____

I am ______________________________

____

I am ______________________________

____

(To be accessible and effective, each must be short, precise and true.)

Positive Thought Builder #3: Write Yourself a Letter

I'll never forget the shock. I got off the GO Train and followed the crowd of commuters away from Union Station. Walking up Yonge Street, I caught a glimpse of my reflection in a store window. I stopped in my tracks, nearly getting run over by the herd hustling to work. *Who is that? That's not me!*

I wear flip-flops and shorts to work. I'm a soccer coach! Where's my whistle? What am I doing wearing a suit? What's with the briefcase? What have I done?! I don't belong here!

The image sticks in my mind because it reflects how I felt when I started my new job as the athletic director at Ryerson—a feeling that lasted almost 18 months. For 15 years, I had been living in a town of only a thousand people, and now I was in charge of a department of 30 at a university with forty thousand full-time students in a city of about 6 million people. I had gone from a budget of $30,000 to over $10 million. I had been hired to take a disastrous athletic program and turn it into a national force. And I had been dropped into an administrative structure that was totally foreign to me: actualization of general ledger codes; cost centers; human resources policies; union guidelines and regulations; university politics and academic plans; and strategic mandate letters with the Ontario Ministry of Training, Colleges and Universities.

I sat in meetings feeling dumb as a post. I'd go home every night and ask Google to help me figure out what was going on. So many times in that first year and a half I had thoughts like: *What am I doing here? I can't do this. I totally blew that meeting. I have no idea what I am doing. I am going to get fired. They are going to find out I don't know anything. This is impossible. I'll never be able to do this. I'm not an administrator. I'm a soccer coach.* Every day, I had a moment when I wanted to push the "easy" button and head back to Iowa, where I was confident and assured—the king of my fiefdom.

So how did I get through it? Polly was there for me, providing the kind of support that we all need. But I had another thing that sustained me: a letter I had written to myself while in Graceland at a high point in my career. My own personal brag sheet. I read that letter so often during the first 18 months of the job that the paper is now as soft as an old flannel shirt. And that's exactly why I wrote it. I outlined my accomplishments so that I could revisit them when things were not going so well. The letter goes like this:

> Dear Ivan,
>
> Congratulations on finding the right woman to marry. Congratulations on raising three healthy and wonderful children and working so hard to spend time with them even when life is busy. You are on track to complete your PhD before you turn 40—nice job. And how about that national championship? You worked hard and believed it could happen and changed those players' lives along the way. Well done. And congratulations on the courage to take the job in Toronto and make the move home. You are following your dream.

The letter isn't about material things or titles; it's about things I did in my life that made me who I am and filled me with confidence in my abilities. It's evidence to remind me that I can get things done, and so I read it when I don't believe I can get anything done. The letter is for those times when the going is pretty rough. When you don't have it all figured out or mastered. When you are new. Or scared.

And the best part is that the letter is in your own voice. It's you being there for you in dark moments when it's hard to remember the good times.

At a time in your life when things are going well, sit down and write a letter to yourself, outlining your hard work and accomplishments. And then keep it on hand so you can pull it out when things are falling apart all around you. To really achieve your full potential, you have to put yourself in situations where you will fail. And when you do, you will find it incredibly helpful to have a comforting word from yourself to combat the hit to your self-confidence.

Positive Thought Builder #4: Reinforce the Behaviors You Want

Coaching, by its very nature, is about correction. In order to help a team or an individual athlete to excel, a coach provides an endless stream of feedback. Part of that process is fixing mistakes. And generations of coaches have been correcting what went wrong for an athlete out loud, in front of the whole team on an ongoing basis: "Sally, the ball went over the net because you were leaning back too far and your head was up. You didn't follow through," and so on. When we focus on the mechanical fix to the problem (e.g., bend your foot this way, change the angle of your arm, turn like this instead of like that), we think we're giving helpful direction. But in many cases, and sometimes more obviously

CATCH THEM WHEN THEY'RE GOOD.

with women's teams than men's, you'll see an athlete wilt in response to the feedback. Their shoulders go down or their head drops. Sure, they'll pick up the ball again. They want to play. They want to succeed. But in that little moment, the coach put a dent in their belief in themselves.

It doesn't have to be that way.

Early in my career, I read a book called *Catch Them Being Good: Everything You Need to Know to Successfully Coach Girls* by Tony DiCicco and Colleen Hacker, who is a sports psychologist and former soccer coach for the U.S. Women's National Team. The book's core message is to emphasize the positive when giving feedback in order to build confidence and see the best behaviors repeated. Instead of constantly pointing to flaws, the idea is to find any evidence you can of the habit you want to reinforce and point that out. In doing so, you will create a culture where athletes who want to excel get positive affirmation from the coach and can learn from observation. They can see which behaviors you want and try to replicate them. That's how you create a climate where learning occurs without put-downs.

EMPHASIZE THE POSITIVE WHEN GIVING FEEDBACK

In one university study, researchers did an experiment with a Division I basketball team to test the role of positive feedback through video analysis. Initially the coaches held a video session in which errors were pointed out to help the players improve. After this error-focused intervention, there was a moderate improvement in the team's performance. Later, the researchers looked at an entirely different approach. Footage was taken again, but the follow-up video session was entirely positive, only pointing at and describing what the players had done right. The coaches basically ignored errors and instead drew the team's attention to the successful moments. If a player had been beaten badly on defense, a coach would point to another part of the video to show how someone had boxed out well. As a result of the second approach, the team's performance improved dramatically. That's the power of positive reinforcement.

When I learned about this approach, it changed the way I parented, coached and led. I started to draw attention to the behaviors I wanted to see repeated. Like in the case of one of my daughters, who is just like me—we both have the attention span of a gnat. After she finishes her milk, the empty glass disappears from her view. It no longer exists. Or the fridge door is left wide open. Or the clothes she changes out of are scattered around the house. I used to nag her to take care of her things. Now I do my best Foghorn Leghorn impersonation and celebrate when something goes right. If she actually puts her dishes in the dishwasher, I'll say, "Gather round, family! I do declare, a miracle has happened! Claire put her dishes away." I try to make it fun and funny. She goes, "Daaaaaaad!" But it puts the spotlight on the right place and positive changes start to happen.

➤ WRITING PROMPT

Identify one person who you acknowledge you have been negative with:

Now, in the coming week, make efforts to change your feedback and catch them when they're good. Watch what happens!

I do the same at work. I comment on the good stuff all the time. Sure, you can't *only* take this approach, because there are some errors and miscues that you have to address. I try to make it 80/20: about 80 percent of the time I'll comment on what is going right. And it works. People get better. You reinforce the approach you want and people come to believe in their own abilities to improve and excel. It's a technique you can use when helping others, but it's also an approach you can use to build your own self-confidence: focus on what went well so it happens more often. Did you work out? Did you refrain from a knee-jerk reaction to something your boss said? Did you get your report in a day early? Did you speak up in a meeting when you had an idea about how to change the company's direction? Celebrate yourself.

CHAPTER 3 RECAP

The Skill of Positive Thought

Positive Thought Builder #1: Stop Negative Thoughts

Use a physical or mental cue to shut out a negative thought and replace it with the belief that you can succeed.

Positive Thought Builder #2: Use Affirmations

Recite a personal value or positive belief you hold about yourself.

Positive Thought Builder #3: Write Yourself a Letter

Outline your accomplishments to revisit when facing tough times.

Positive Thought Builder #4: Reinforce the Behaviors You Want

Reinforce positive behaviors rather than focusing on mistakes.

4

SELECT EXCELLENCE

THE SKILL OF TEAM BUILDING

"I can do things you cannot, you can do things I cannot; together we can do great things."

MOTHER TERESA

WHEN I WAS coaching soccer at Graceland, I always had the ultimate accomplishment in mind: help my players develop the confidence and skill necessary to win a national title. It was a single-minded pursuit, and I left no stone unturned. I broke into the stadium at night to water the grass after I was told not to. I moved outdoor soccer goals inside a gym so we could have proper shooting practice during cold weather. I held training sessions at 11:00 on Sunday nights because it was the only time field space was free. I did everything I could think of to create the best possible soccer program. And when we did win the championship, the entire town came out for the parade. But it wasn't all ticker tape and pats on the back.

My big dreams and unconventional methods weren't popular with the majority of the university's administration and with a variety of rule-obsessed folks around campus. In fact, I think my supervisor—Dean of Students Tom

Powell—regularly received complaints about my creative approaches to getting students engaged. To this day, I am sure that if Tom had not been such a huge supporter, I would have been fired long before my team won it all. It wasn't a stretch for Tom to support me because he was my mentor. He taught me what he called the "ministry of presence": being with the students as often and as genuinely as possible to ensure they had an exceptional experience. I tried to live this out as best as I could. But when the victory parade was over, the same old routine of people rejecting my ideas started up again.

There was increasing conflict between me and the leadership who, from my perspective, were resisting just for the sake of resisting. I was setting new goals, but there was almost no support for those goals or for me. It got harder and harder to stay positive, until Polly and I eventually had another one of those conversations about not letting anyone else decide what I could and could not do. So I started to look for work elsewhere. It was a *huge* decision. Polly had grown up in Iowa; our kids were born there. Leaving would be very hard. But we decided that it was time.

Soon after, a headhunter invited me to interview for a position at Ryerson University in Toronto. Initially, I wasn't exactly thrilled because Ryerson didn't have a great reputation. (When I was young, it did very poorly in sports and was known as "Rye High" because it was more like a community college than a university.) But the job was back home in Ontario, so I went for the interview. What I discovered at

Ryerson is something that the entire country now knows but didn't in 2008: the visionary and enterprising leadership of now-former President Sheldon Levy was turning Ryerson into a whole new school.

At my interview, the Ryerson team asked me typical questions based on case studies and explored my leadership style and approach to change. They also spent some time outlining their ambitious plans for the Athletics Department. I remember thinking that I wasn't really suitable for the position given what they wanted to accomplish. But Sheldon and the provost, Alan Shepard, saw something in me that they liked, and the feeling was mutual. They offered me the job, and I accepted. And when I moved my family to Canada, I found myself working in an incredibly supportive environment with people who not only wanted me to succeed but who were highly committed to innovation and entrepreneurship.

From the time I started at Ryerson until December of 2015 when Sheldon left to become Deputy Minister of the Ministry of Training, Colleges and Universities (now the Ministry of Advanced Education and Skills Development), I was inspired and exhilarated by him. He was an incredible mentor for me and we got along brilliantly. Whenever we met, we would share ideas and discuss the long-term vision for the university. His favorite quote about city building is from American architect Daniel Burnham: "Make no little plans. They have no magic to stir men's blood and probably themselves will not be realized. Make big plans; aim high in

"A group becomes a team when each member is sure enough of himself and his contribution to praise the skill of the others."

NORMAN S. HIDLE

hope and work." And every time we met, Sheldon would ask me, "What do you need? How can I help?" He was endlessly supportive. And it made all the difference to my career.

Tom Powell and Sheldon Levy are two among a handful of people I have worked with who were totally committed to supporting my growth. Through them, I learned more than ever before that a key component in building self-confidence is to surround yourself with people who believe in you. I call this the skill of team building because it requires mental discipline and effort to find the right people and leave the wrong ones behind. It's easy to go with the flow and not be too choosy about your relationships and companions. It's a lot harder to know what you need and be deliberate and conscious about finding it. This can involve trial and error and making difficult choices, like leaving a job or letting old acquaintances drop away. But you can develop the skill of team building if you stay focused on what matters: keep people in your life who are committed to your success, and let people who demoralize you go. This is how you select excellence.

The Skill of Team Building

"Talent wins games, but teamwork and intelligence win championships." MICHAEL JORDAN

To build your self-confidence—your unwavering belief in yourself—you need an encouraging environment where you can try new things, sometimes fail and sometimes succeed, and never worry whether you will be supported. In your personal life and work, look for a team that values you and will encourage your learning and living. Why? Because the people around us have a big effect on us. Research shows that we are hugely influenced by the five people we spend the most time with. Think about your five people. Not your *favorite* five people (although no doubt they're pretty awesome), but the people you spend the most time with. Now ask yourself: Do they understand you? Do they support you? Do they recognize your achievements and encourage you when you fail? If one or two of them don't, you've got the wrong team. Ask yourself if you can select better.

FAMOUS FAILURE

Bill Belichick was fired from his job as head coach of the newly formed Baltimore Ravens in February of 1996 and did not return to a head coaching job until 2000, when he took over the New England Patriots.

There's a reason why the history of sports includes so much mythology about exceptional teams, and why there are so many examples of successful people who have bonded with other successful people. In both cases, they are fueling each other to be better. There are obvious amazing partnerships like Lennon and McCartney or Damon and Affleck, but there are also less well-known examples that are equally inspiring. Ray Kroc and Walt Disney found each other in the middle of World War I when they were both ambulance drivers—long before Kroc went on to found

McDonald's and before Disney established one of the most successful creative enterprises of all time. Authors Truman Capote and Harper Lee knew each other from childhood and supported each other as they became two of the greatest American writers of their generation. Finding people who make you better is not an accident: we bump into thousands of people throughout our lives. We need to hold on to the ones who help us to become more, which then builds our self-confidence.

Team-Builder #1: Seek People Who Value Creativity

Parenting is a great example of the importance of creating an environment that makes failure okay. Kids need to be supported and not judged for getting something wrong. Accountability and responsibility are important, but hammering kids when they flop teaches them to not even try. They need to see failures as learning opportunities, not catastrophes. The same goes for adults. We need supportive friends, colleagues, spouses, bosses and clients who will embrace our ambition and recognize that failure is a side effect of innovation. Creative people drop the ball sometimes. And we all make bad choices occasionally that put us on the wrong path. This is life. It needs to be okay to fail as part of becoming a person who succeeds more often than not.

One of the best examples I have seen of this approach is the Digital Media Zone (DMZ) at Ryerson. An incubator for start-up businesses, the DMZ was one of the first and most successful campus-based accelerators for young entrepreneurs trying to turn their bright ideas into successful ventures. In less than five years, it advanced from an idea to being the number-one campus-based accelerator in North America and number three in the world. The motto at the DMZ is "fail fast." The program encourages young thinkers and leaders to go gangbusters in translating their ideas into marketplace ventures so they quickly discover if their idea will work. The premise is that there is no learning quite like learning from failure, and the entrepreneurs at the DMZ have a different attitude toward failure because of the climate around them.

When it comes to personal confidence, we need people close by who will be there for us when we crash and burn. We all lose our way sometimes. We make decisions that don't turn out well. We might even get knocked down and need someone to help us up. For me, Polly is my number-one support. Whenever I make a mess, she helps me understand what happened and how to put the pieces back together. When I was at Graceland, one of my closest colleagues and best friends was Kevin Prine, a professor whose entrepreneurial center on campus produced a team that won the national championship at the Students in Free Enterprise (SIFE) USA National Exposition. Kevin and I were the only two faculty members to bring Graceland a national

GET AWAY FROM PEOPLE **WHO TEAR** YOU DOWN.

championship, and we supported each other all the way along. And I've already mentioned Tom Powell and Sheldon Levy—leaders who encouraged me to dream big and were understanding if I made a mess.

Of course, the flip side is also true. You have to get away from people who will tear you down. We've all been in situations with leaders, colleagues and teammates who resist innovation and are poisonous to our dreams. If this happens to you, do everything you can to make a change; otherwise your belief in yourself will drain away. None of us can thrive in a toxic setting.

➤ WRITING PROMPT

Can you identify five people who tear you down or who put boundaries on your success?

1 ______

2 ______

3 ______

4 ______

5 ______

What steps will you take to limit your interactions with these people?

____

____

____

____

____

Team Builder #2: Surround Yourself with the Best

In 1968, a young man named Bruce Jenner arrived at Graceland University on a partial football scholarship. In his freshman year, Jenner injured his knee and had to stop playing football. At the suggestion of his coach, L.D. Weldon, he took up decathlon and achieved enough success to make it onto the national team and qualify for the 1972 Olympics in Munich. While there, a moment occurred that changed the course of Jenner's life.

He was warming up near the track when Bert Bonanno, a coach from San José City College and the head coach of the Peruvian track team, walked over and said hello. Bonanno asked the athlete what his plans were for training

"I remember early in my career with Disney, which was a very strange time in the company—there were a couple of executives who were very supportive of me and kind of let me do my own thing."

TIM BURTON

once he got back to the United States, and Jenner explained that he was returning to Iowa to finish his studies. Bonanno invited him to come to San José, California, as that's where many of the world's best track-and-field athletes were training. After that brief conversation, Jenner finished 10th in the decathlon and Bonanno didn't hear from him again. Then, in the summer of 1973, Jenner suddenly showed up at the San José City College training facility. In an interview later in his life with the San José *Mercury News*, Jenner said, "As soon as I took off my cap and gown, I jumped into my '63 Volkswagen bug. Pole vault strapped to the roof. Javelins sticking out the doors. Headed west. I asked myself, 'Where are the world's greatest athletes training?' That's why I picked San José."

Jenner's training in San José is the stuff of track-and-field legend: eight-hour training sessions, hustling for money, working at night selling insurance, taking his golden retriever everywhere and going for pineapple milkshakes at Dairy Queen after training sessions. He was so well-known that large crowds would come to watch him train and fans even brought him porterhouse steaks. But it was the other athletes who drew Jenner there and made his time such a success. The area was known as "Speed City" because of all the runners who trained at San José State University under famous sprinting coach Bud Winter, but it was also known as "Strength City" for the throwers who trained with Bonanno. For Jenner, who had to perfect his technique in 10 different events, being with the best of every sport was the perfect training ground. He went on to become the world-record holder and Olympic gold medalist in the decathlon at the 1976 Olympics in Montreal. He also became one of the most famous athletes of his time. All because he knew enough to train with the best in the world.

Fast-forward almost 40 years to Jenner's high-profile transition from Bruce to Caitlyn, and we can see further evidence of incredible confidence. Caitlyn is now a leader in the movement for tolerance, understanding and diversity, who speaks widely on transgender issues and consults with organizations like the United Nations. She has shown that if you have a deep belief in yourself and are surrounded by love and support, you can pursue your dreams. To improve your life and boost your confidence, make sure you surround yourself with the best.

➤ WRITING PROMPT

Can you identify five people who build you up and who support your personal and professional growth?

1 ______________________________

2 ______________________________

3 ______________________________

4 __________

5 __________

How will you engage these people to grow and nurture these relationships?

____

____

____

____

Team Builder #3: Create a Culture of Excellence

In addition to the individuals you surround yourself with, your belief in yourself is strongly influenced by the groups you belong to. This is the reason that sports teams talk so much about culture. They want to create an environment where it's normal for everyone to behave like a champion, on and off the field. A "good enough" culture is the kiss of death for high performance and will undermine your growth. It's nearly impossible to excel in a climate that isn't firmly committed to being the best. That's why most experienced coaches will tell you that you should never keep a high-performing athlete on your team if they are bad for team culture and cohesion. If you keep them based on their individual performance and ignore the negative effect they have on the team, you invite ongoing difficulties and limit the success of your group. Great coaches make the tough call and get rid of those players, even if they're incredibly talented. Culture is too important to ignore.

A good illustration of the importance of overall culture was when the leaders of the Canadian Olympic Committee (COC) decided to change the perception that Canadian teams would always excel in hockey and curling but would struggle to win consistently in other sports. With the Own the Podium initiative, the leadership at the COC created a culture where it was expected that Canadian athletes would win. And it worked. By the time the Winter Olympics in Vancouver arrived, the COC had openly expressed its intention to win the medal count. When those Games were over, they had fallen just short of that goal, but Canada had more gold medals than any other nation. And when Sidney Crosby

BRING PEOPLE INTO YOUR LIFE WHO ARE COMMITTED TO YOUR SUCCESS.

SURROUND YOURSELF WITH **PEOPLE WHO BELIEVE IN YOU.**

scored the Golden Goal, it was the first time in the history of the Winter Games that any country had won 14 gold medals.

Another example of the importance of having a winning culture can be seen in how New Zealand approaches rugby. Despite having a population of only 4 million people, New Zealand boasts one of the greatest sports dynasties ever: the All Blacks. The program is the winningest international rugby Test side in the history of the sport, having won 75 percent of their matches since 1903, which is the best record for *any* international sport. And in October of 2015, when New Zealand won the Rugby World Cup, it became the only nation to win the championship in back-to-back years.

What makes New Zealand unique is not just its obsession with rugby but the extraordinary culture of the All Blacks. Players think of the team as a religion or a philosophy, not just a jersey they pull on before they play. For years, there was a secret black book that listed the primary guidelines for living like an All Black—all of which, when the book finally became public, are essentially about setting near-impossible standards. Team members use phrases like "An All Black is always in search of the perfect game," "An All Black says, 'I'm never good enough'" and "Being an All Black is bigger than you." Through their fundamental beliefs, they create a culture where everyone elevates their performance all the time. And while you may not live in an environment as extreme as the All Black culture, you can look for and help to create a culture around you where success is the only option.

CHAPTER 4 RECAP

The Skill of Team Building

Team Builder #1: Seek People Who Value Creativity
Friends, family and colleagues who value experimentation and improvement will support you along the way.

Team Builder #2: Surround Yourself with the Best
High-achievers in the areas of work and life you most value will make you better.

Team Builder #3: Create a Culture of Excellence
Help to build an environment where everyone involved wants to elevate their performance.

5

GET UP AGAIN

THE SKILL OF GRIT

"Success is not final, failure is not fatal: it is the courage to continue that counts."

WINSTON CHURCHILL

I REMEMBER IT LIKE it was yesterday. A young man named Kyle came up to me before the men's soccer team tryouts one year at Ryerson. He said, "Coach, I've read *The Secret*. I've got Ryerson Rams tickets on my dream board. I want to play for you. I know you won a national championship in Iowa." I love a guy with conviction, so I said, "Okay, Kyle. Come on out." So he came to the tryout and played. And he was terrible. Oh man. A couple of floors below terrible. And after the tryouts he asked, "How did I do, Coach?" All I could say was, "Um... Kyle... how would you like to be our equipment manager?" He was crestfallen. But he said, "Okay, okay." He took the job and the season started. And like any other coach who tries to help a kid, I put him in every now and then, if we were winning by a lot or if I knew the game would be easy for us. His foot was made of rubber: the ball bounced left, the ball bounced right. Pretty much anywhere except where he intended. But he played.

When the season ended, I did exit interviews with each of the players. We talked about how they did and what they needed to work on in the off-season. Then in came Kyle. The equipment manager arrives for an exit interview. I didn't want to hurt his feelings, so I stumbled through it: "I... um... you folded the pinnies good... you blew up the balls." What was I supposed to say? I tried to be nice. And then he put me on the spot: "Coach, what do I need to do to get better?" I thought about it for a bit. I knew I needed to be genuine with him because he cared so much about making the team. I said, "Well, Kyle, to be honest... you can't do a thousand keep-ups, your feet are really, really stiff and you aren't very strong." He sat there for a minute and then he said, "Yah, but Coach, you know, I think I can do those things." That's when I realized that I was going to have to be really blunt with him: "Kyle, you've got the feet of a goat. You are not going to make it. You've got three All-Canadian center-backs in front of you. I mean, if all three of them went down with an injury, maybe then you'd have a chance to sit on the end of the bench." I figured that was pretty clear. And I was probably crushing the kid. But what did Kyle hear? "So, you're saying there's a chance?" I kid you not. I was thinking, *You will never make this team in a million years.* But I didn't say that to him; I just laid out his chances. And he walked off thinking he had a shot. Talk about conviction!

The next year—this is year two—Kyle showed up to tryouts with his soccer boots on. He'd been lifting weights and running. He played awesome—for Kyle. He played a lot

"I have not failed. I've just found 10,000 ways that won't work."

THOMAS EDISON

better! But guess what? He didn't make the team. No happy ending. He was devastated. But at least it was over.

When the third year rolled around, we knew before the season started that we needed center midfielders (which wasn't Kyle's position). I called a local club coach I knew: "Do you have any center midfielders?" He said "Yah, I got a couple of guys" and sent me three players. They arrived for the first tryout, and guess what? In walked Kyle and two others. Under my breath I was like, "Doggone it, bloody heck!" But then I thought, *Okay, Ivan, just relax. Humor him. No harm in that*. So he tried out again, but he still just wasn't good enough. The other guys were though. I didn't want to cut Kyle again in front of the other players, so I talked to the whole team, even the returning players who I knew I'd be keeping, and said, "Thank you, guys. You all did a nice job, but I'm only going to keep a certain number of you. I'll give you a call to let you know."

Soon after, I was on the bus with a squad of players from the previous year traveling to Syracuse for an exhibition game. I went to call the other guys who came out with Kyle to tell them they made the team—without realizing I had mixed up the phone numbers. When a player answered, I explained that I wanted him to play in an upcoming game against Guelph University. He said, "I'll be there! Thanks, Coach. Thanks, Coach. All right. Just shoot me an e-mail of the schedule." I said, "Okay, what's your address?" "It's Kyle dot..." Inside my head I was like, *Noooooo! Sugar sticks!* I hung up the phone thinking, *What can I do? What can I do? Well, he's on the team now, but he's not going to play. I'll put him in a uniform. It's going to make his day. He's going to sit on the bench, but he will be on the team.*

So Kyle came to the game and he sat on the bench. And then it happened. One center-back went down. A second center-back went down. The third center-back went down. So Kyle ended up playing and, lo and behold, he was phenomenal! The best player on my team by a long shot. Not only did he play in that game, he played every game for the rest of the season. We went undefeated and ended up being number two in the country—the highest ranking ever for Ryerson. And when we played at the national championship, guess who was the starting center-back? Kyle. Now, as I write this, three years later, Kyle is an Academic All-Canadian and an Ontario University Athletics all-star—one of the top 11 university soccer players in Ontario.

"So... you're saying there's a chance?"

Watch a video about this remarkable young man by searching "Kyle Stewart: Chances" on YouTube

The Skill of Grit

"You may encounter many defeats, but you must not be defeated. In fact, it may be necessary to encounter the defeats, so you can know who you are, what you can rise from, how you can still come out of it." MAYA ANGELOU

Grit is mental toughness and courage. It is the ability to sustain interest in and effort toward very long-term and particularly challenging goals. Angela Duckworth, an American

"Success is stumbling from failure to failure with no loss of enthusiasm."

WINSTON CHURCHILL

psychologist at the University of Pennsylvania, is a world leader in the study of grit. In essence, Duckworth studies what it takes for a person to dream big and never quit. Before attending grad school, she was a math and science teacher in a low-income neighborhood, where she observed that the students who excelled weren't necessarily the brightest, but they were almost always the ones who never quit. They had a capacity to stick with something and endure setbacks that separated them from their less successful peers. If they failed, they tried again.

Duckworth went on to become a leading researcher in the area and, beginning in 2004, she and several colleagues developed a 12-item self-response questionnaire to measure grit. Eventually her team was invited to work with the leaders at the world-famous United States Military Academy, known commonly as West Point, to develop an effective predictor of which candidates would stick with the program. Despite having one of the most rigorous admission processes in the world, West Point found that 1 in 20 of their freshmen dropped out before the first summer was over. So Duckworth and her team set out to draw a correlation between a student's grit score and their success during "Beast Barracks," the seven-week-long Cadet Basic Training. In the end, they found that grit—basically, determination plus perseverance—was a more accurate predictor of success than any of the instruments West Point had been using.

Duckworth and her research associates ran a similar study at the 2005 Scripps National Spelling Bee, the world's largest spelling competition for children from across the United States. They discovered that it wasn't intellectual abilities like memory or language skill that led to success, but grit. Since then, Duckworth and her team have gone on to demonstrate that grit is an emotional and mental quality required for success in almost any setting.

I also consider grit a prerequisite for self-confidence, because I have learned from experience that people who quit early or who can't handle setbacks never develop a basic belief in their ability to accomplish things. But you can learn to stick with things. You can practice perseverance. Like all the others, grit is a skill learned through repetition. And when you acquire more of it, your belief in yourself rises and you are another step closer to being a person of high self-confidence.

Grit Builder #1: Believe You Can Change

Carol Dweck is a renowned psychologist from Stanford University who wrote a seminal work called *Mindset: The New Psychology of Success*. In it, Dweck outlines the key idea of her research: A person's *view* of their ability to improve has a huge effect on their *actual* ability to improve. If you have a growth mindset—the belief that ability, intelligence and personality can improve—you will continually progress and excel. If you have a fixed mindset—the belief that abilities are inborn and cannot change—you will conclude that you can't grow your intelligence and will have a tendency to give up when things get tough. Failure is a sign of being stupid, and stupid is something you can't change, so what's the point of carrying on? So believeth the fixed-mindsetters.

In one study, Dweck and her colleagues organized seventh graders in a New York City public school into two groups: those who showed a growth mindset and those who demonstrated a fixed mindset. The researchers then provided feedback that reinforced the students' existing concept of intelligence. The fixed-mindset kids were told "You got it right because you are smart" (as if "smart" is something you just "are"), while the growth-mindset kids were given feedback that was about effort, not intelligence: "You worked hard and that's why you found a solution." The researchers then monitored academic progress of both groups of students for two years. The results were significant. Students with a fixed mindset—even the very intelligent ones—struggled with achievement and were more likely to give up in the face of a challenge and conclude they were no longer smart. They believed that intelligence was something they either had or didn't have—and if they couldn't do something, it meant they didn't have it, so why even try? The kids with a growth mindset stuck with problems longer and had much-improved results. They believed that effort and persistence would lead to success. They stuck with difficult problems and as a result, they got smarter and better.

What you believe really does affect what you accomplish. It becomes a self-fulfilling prophecy. If you believe you can't grow your intelligence, you won't. You'll give up when things become hard. But with a growth mindset, you will see setbacks as opportunities for greater progress. And you will also locate the power to excel right where it should be—inside of you.

Grit Builder #2: Praise the Process

A second finding in Dweck's work focuses on the role of feedback. If you praise a person for their talent or intelligence, they begin to fear that these qualities lie outside their control—again, as things they either "have" or "don't have." They actually *develop* a fixed mindset, focusing on how smart they are and worrying like heck that they're going to hit their limit and eventually be dumb. It seems like a good idea to call someone smart, but Dweck's research tells us that it makes people anxious, that they feel they cannot control it and that they lose confidence in themselves. But if you praise a person for their effort—something they can control—you enforce their belief that they are the power behind their success. After all, effort is visible and measurable, and a person can do more of it any time they like. As Dweck puts it, "When you praise kids' intelligence and they fail, they think they aren't smart anymore, and they lose interest in their work. In contrast, kids praised for effort show no impairment and often are energized in the face of difficulty."

Change the way you think about your ability, and you change the way you think about failure. You come to see challenges as opportunities. That's why Kyle was so

FOCUS

FOCUS

ON THE

FOCUS

PROCESS—

FOCUS

NOT THE

OUTCOME.

successful in trying out for the soccer team. He simply would not interpret the feedback I gave him as evidence that he could not improve. He believed in effort and growth. Another kid would have told himself, *I guess I just don't have the talent*, and quit. Kyle thought, *I just need to work harder and I'll get there.*

WRITING PROMPT

Think of a project you worked on recently. List three things you did during the process that went well, no matter what the outcome was:

1 ____

2 ____

3 ____

Grit Builder #3: Try Something Hard and Stick to It

Learning from failure means being in situations where you can fail. I don't just mean doing something that doesn't go exactly as you had hoped. I mean getting involved in a project or challenge that matters to you. That way, you can learn to cope with the emotions that come with failure. Start slowly with small-scale projects and build up to ones with big emotional stakes. Along the way, you'll build up the resilience you need to believe in yourself.

It's also important to stick with situations. Constantly switching from challenge to challenge and leaving when the going gets tough is another way to chip away at your resilience. My wife and I learned this firsthand with our son, who is a great athlete but who has difficulty as a student. Learning is a constant struggle for him. So while we worked with his teachers to help him succeed academically, we also moved him around from sport to sport so he could "find his thing." Our intention was to offset his sensation of failure in school with a sensation of success in sport. But our efforts ended up undermining his belief in himself because he never stayed in one activity for very long. He began to believe he couldn't succeed or persevere, which is the opposite of what we set out to achieve. Eventually, we stopped moving him around and left him on the swim team, which was the right move. Now, if his times aren't fast enough and the coach is correcting his technique, he gets to figure out how to fix it by sticking with it. He owns the success and he owns the failure. And his attitude about himself is gradually changing, in sport and in school. By allowing him to stick with it, we are helping him build his belief that he can succeed.

FAMOUS FAILURE

Abraham Lincoln suffered several political defeats before finally being elected President in 1860.

CHAPTER 5 RECAP

The Skill of Grit

Grit Builder #1: Believe You Can Change
Adopt a growth mindset in which you believe you can improve your mental capacities.

Grit Builder #2: Praise the Process
Provide positive feedback to yourself and others based on effort and commitment, not on talent and outcomes.

Grit Builder #3: Try Something Hard and Stick to It
Accept a challenge just beyond your current capability and see it through to the end—no matter the outcome.

6

STRIVE FOR MORE

THE SKILL OF HIGHER EXPECTATIONS

"Big results require big ambitions."

HERACLITUS

WHEN I FIRST starting coaching soccer, I made a commitment to myself and to my players that fitness was going to be a key part of our success. Any player who wanted to play for me, no matter how talented, had to run two miles in under 12 minutes. That's eight laps around a 400-meter track—a version of the Cooper test developed for military fitness in the late 1960s. I told the players well in advance, gave them time to prepare to meet the standard and then tested them at the start of training camp. If they didn't make it, I gave them a few chances over the course of the two weeks, but if they couldn't do it by the end, they were off the team.

Whenever we ran the test, there would be one or two guys who came in at 10:05 or 10:06 on the stopwatch, and then the rest of the team would squeak in at 11:57, 11:58, 11:59. It was always the same. They were just meeting the criteria. Over the years, I realized I was doing the same thing over and over again and expecting a different result—fitter players.

So I eventually changed the fitness standards. Instead of 12 minutes, I told the players they were going to have to run the two miles in 11:30 to make the team. Sure enough, that year the same two guys came in at 10:05 and 10:06 and then every other player came in at 11:27, 11:28, 11:29, 11:30. I'm thinking, *Huh! I'm on to something. I'm no dummy.* So the next year, I made the cut-off time 11 minutes. And guess what? 10:05, 10:06 for one or two... then 10:57, 10:58, 10:59 for the rest of them. By this point, I'm thinking, *What the heck, 10:30. I'm going to make it 10:30!* So I did. And the next year, the stragglers came in at 10:27, 10:28, 10:29. If you don't know sport, 10:30 is getting up there in terms of speed. But every single player met the minimum expectations I set. I didn't lower the time any further, but from then on, that was the time that every player got and still gets to this day.

What I realized is that improving an athlete's performance is actually about changing the way they think about their success. By raising the minimum expectation, I made the entire team faster. So I thought, *I'm a professor—I wonder if this can work for academic performance?* And sure enough, it did. Working from the minimum 2.0 GPA required by the National Collegiate Athletic Association and the National Association of Intercollegiate Athletics, I started to raise the expectations for what a player had to achieve in the classroom in order to be on the team. When I set it at 2.25, many of my players turned in 2.26, 2.27, 2.28. When I raised it to 2.50, those same kids got 2.51, 2.52. 2.53. And when I raised it to 2.75, they posted 2.76, 2.77, 2.78. They improved their performance because the expectations were higher.

PEOPLE WILL RISE

TO YOUR MINIMUM LEVEL OF EXPECTATION—

SET THE BAR HIGH.

Hans the Horse

In the late 1800s, Charles Darwin's claims that humans descended from apes led to widespread interest in animal intelligence. People wanted to know just how smart animals are. So a retired German school teacher named Wilhelm von Osten decided he was going to try to teach three animals to count: a kitten, a bear cub and his own horse, Hans. For over two years, von Osten painstakingly worked to help the animals learn to count. How? He used basic techniques like holding their paw or hoof in his hand and stomping it on the ground a certain number of times when he showed them a number. In time, Hans the horse began to demonstrate enormous abilities, including spelling on a board using large letters of the alphabet and even performing arithmetic. Hans's talent was so stunning and impressive that von Osten traveled around Germany showing off the animal. Interest in the horse grew so significantly that not only was there a *New York Times* article written about him, the German authorities established a panel to investigate the situation, which included a veterinarian, a circus manager, a cavalry officer, several teachers and the director of the Berlin Zoological Garden.

In a 1904 report, the commission concluded that there were no tricks involved in the performance: Hans could count and spell. Unsatisfied with that result, the government passed the investigation to psychologist Oskar Pfungst, who tested Hans under research conditions such as having someone else ask the questions or putting blinders on the horse. Initially, Pfungst determined that for Hans to answer a question correctly, two conditions had to be in place. First, the questioner had to know the answer to the question. Second, Hans had to be able to see the questioner. But why? By studying the questioners in great detail, Pfungst discovered that as the horse got close to the answer, the questioner would display subtle tells such as raised eyebrows, changes in posture, narrowing eyes. And then, when the horse finally arrived at the right answer, the tension in the questioner would be released and an expression of relief would spread over their entire body. Hans was picking up physical and emotional cues.

Based on this research, psychologists developed an understanding of what is called "the Clever Hans effect," an observer-expectancy effect whereby the expectations of a researcher will skew the responses of the subject of a study. Which is a roundabout way of saying we are highly responsive to even the slightest shift in other people's expectations of us.

INCREASED EXPECTATIONS LEAD TO IMPROVED PERFORMANCE.

"High achievement always takes place in the framework of high expectations."

JACK KINDER

The Skill of Higher Expectations

"Every great dream begins with a dreamer. Always remember, you have within you the strength, the patience and the passion to reach for the stars to change the world."
HARRIET TUBMAN

Do you remember *My Fair Lady*, in which lower-class Cockney flower girl Eliza Doolittle learns how to speak the Queen's English? What about the movie *Trading Places*, where Eddie Murphy goes from being a homeless thief to a successful stockbroker? Both stories are about the role that expectations play in determining behavior. They are also examples of a widely known psychological phenomenon called the Pygmalion effect, which was first discovered in 1968 by researchers Robert Rosenthal and Lenore Jacobson when they set out to assess the impact of teacher expectations on student performance.

After assessing the intelligence of students in a California elementary school—without the students knowing that this was the nature of the test they took—the researchers gave the teachers the names of students who had "unusual potential for academic growth" and who could be expected to bloom during the year. The twist was that this group of students was selected entirely at random and not based on test scores. The "high-potential" kids were just a cross section of the larger group. When the researchers returned eight months later and performed the intelligence test again, they found that the students who'd been labeled as having significant potential scored much higher on the intelligence test than they did the first time around.

Rosenthal and Jacobson concluded that when teachers had higher expectations for particular students, those students performed better. Why? Because when a teacher believes that a student can succeed, they are more likely to provide feedback, attention, support and positive reinforcement, all of which leads students to not only perform better but to feel better about their ability. As a result, the student is more likely to believe they can succeed and to keep working at finding a solution to a problem. It's a reinforced cycle: increased expectations lead to increased performance.

Learning to meet our own higher expectations, and not just those expressed by others, is also a skill we can teach ourselves. No one is born with an innate ability to raise their own standards. But we can all learn the role that expectations play and the best way to set them for ourselves. And then, of course, we can practice. Self-confidence grows when we realize that we can set—and are capable of meeting—higher expectations.

Higher Expectations Builder #1: Believe You Can Do It

On a May morning in 1954, a 25-year-old English medical student named Roger Bannister took a train from London and headed for the University of Oxford. Bannister was one of the fastest middle-distance runners in the world. He was returning to his alma mater to compete on behalf of the Amateur Athletic Association of England's team against Oxford's track club in a dual meet event. But it wasn't just any old race. Bannister intended to break the speed barrier by running a sub-four-minute mile. Middle-distance runners all over the world, including Bannister, had been attempting to break the record for years and it was widely believed to be impossible.

FAMOUS FAILURE

J.K. Rowling was rejected 12 times before a publisher agreed to pick up *Harry Potter and the Philosopher's Stone*.

Despite the wet and windy conditions that day, Bannister arrived and made preparations to run. Leading up to the race, he had been using intervals to improve his foot speed and had developed a plan to use two teammates to pace him for half of the race. When the gun went off, Bannister took off, with future Commonwealth Games gold medalist Chris Chataway pacing him. Then, when Chataway tired, he signaled to Chris Brasher—a future Olympic gold medalist—to take over. As they got within 200 meters of the finish, Bannister poured it on and raced to victory. But had he done it?

After the results were finalized, the stadium announcer gave a long, drawn-out, excitement-building announcement of the nationally and internationally broadcast event: "Ladies and gentlemen, here is the result of event nine, the one mile: first, number 41, R.G. Bannister, Amateur Athletic Association and formerly of Exeter and Merton Colleges,

Oxford, with a time which is a new meet and track record, and which—subject to ratification—will be a new English Native, British National, All-Comers, European, British Empire and World Record. The time was three. . . ." When the first number was announced, the crowd went wild. Bannister had achieved what no one thought was possible. He had run 3:59:40.

My players love this story—an athlete who does something that no one had ever done. But that's not why I tell them about it. I tell them because I want to talk about what happened after he broke through the barrier: the four-minute mile became normal. Increasingly, runners broke that time, often without pacers. These days, high schoolers break that time on a regular basis. Why? Mainly because they know they can. Ultimately, Bannister broke the record because he believed that he could.

Higher Expectations Builder #2: Push for Continual Improvement

One of my favorite historical figures is Leonardo da Vinci, the artist and innovator who did everything from inventing a way for humans to fly to painting the *Mona Lisa*. I have spent hours looking at da Vinci's notebooks and reading about his ideas. He's someone who loved to expand his thinking. And of all his qualities, his insatiable desire to improve lies at the heart of his work, as seen in the hundreds of sketches

“High expectations are the key to everything.”

SAM WALTON

of human anatomy, for example. He never felt he knew enough or was good enough, which, believe it or not, is a quality that confident people share. Confident people aren't afraid to say "I don't really understand" or "I can do better." Remember the All Blacks: "I'm never good enough." And they are exceptional!

Da Vinci's belief resembles the business philosophy Kaizen, an approach often referred to simply as "continuous improvement," which was developed in Japan after World War II. In essence, Kaizen is an organizational philosophy that emphasizes the power of frontline managers and workers to turn problems into opportunities. Unlike the traditional Western mindset "If it ain't broke, don't fix it," the thinking behind Kaizen is essentially "We need to constantly get better so that we can become and stay the best." If you can adopt a continual-improvement mindset, you will be able to set higher expectations for yourself that keep elevating your performance.

Higher Expectations Builder #3: Learn from Feedback

I once coached an incredibly talented player who I will call Luis. He had all kinds of natural gifts: quick feet, loads of endurance, good skills. But he often performed below his potential. He was selfish with the ball. He pressed for opportunities to score when the better option was to be patient and share possession with others. He got frustrated if someone didn't make a pass to him. Eventually, he approached four individuals and asked them for feedback about his play: two assistant coaches, a respected senior player and me. Each one of us independently gave the same message: you are not a good teammate. At first, he was highly resistant and dismissed the idea. But after he had heard the same thing from all of us, something amazing happened. He took the message to heart and he changed overnight. He went from being focused on his own desire to score goals to being focused on supporting the other players. As a result, his opportunities to score actually increased and he put the ball in the net far more than he had previously, while at the same time dramatically improving his teammates' feelings toward him. Not to mention making the team better overall. By accepting feedback he didn't love hearing, he was able to make an instrumental change. This is critical for all of us. We all need people who will give us honest, constructive input about how we are doing, and then we need to accept the information and learn from it.

It may be helpful to know that two types of feedback have the most powerful influence on learning and achievement: feedback on the task (what you have done) and feedback on the process (how you have done it). Any feedback on you as an individual—say, on your personality—is generally not effective. So when you seek feedback from others, ask them what they think about the thing you have done (how did it turn out?) and the way you approached it (could you adjust your method?). Gather data from a few people you trust. Then triangulate the feedback, find the key messages and reflect on ways you can improve. It's about being humble and genuinely accepting that you can do better.

If you can't learn from feedback and make changes, you may find that your team or organization moves on without you. I have seen several situations where an individual's inability to take input from others led to that person being cut from a team or removed from an organization. Being open to feedback and making an authentic effort to change is an essential quality for long-term membership and participation in any team.

➤ WRITING PROMPT

List three people you trust who can give you honest feedback about some aspect of your performance—either in general or regardng a particular role/task/project.

1 ____________________

2 ____________________

3 ____________________

Now arrange to ask each of them for their input and then triangulate the feedback.

CHAPTER 6 RECAP

The Skill of Higher Expectations

Higher Expectations Builder #1: Believe You Can Do It

Even if something seems too difficult or out of reach, begin moving toward it with a belief that it is possible.

Higher Expectations Builder #2: Push for Continual Improvement

Never think things are as good as they can get; commit to small, ongoing improvements.

Higher Expectations Builder #3: Learn from Feedback

Seek feedback from honest and insightful people about how you can improve, and take their message to heart.

7

PAY ATTENTION

THE SKILL OF FOCUS

"To be everywhere is to be nowhere."

SENECA

WHEN I TEACH corporate teams how to improve their performance, I put them through an exercise called The Maze. I divide the group in half and ask each side to come up with a fun team name. I then use masking tape to create a maze on the floor that is basically a large grid like a chessboard, usually ten-by-ten, which the participants watch me create without knowing what it is for. When I have finished, I explain that they are looking at a maze and that there is a secret path through the maze, which the two teams have to figure out how to get everyone through. I further explain that the two teams will start at opposite ends and take turns sending one member at a time through to attempt to discover the route. And whenever a person makes a false move when stepping from square to square, trying to find and memorize the invisible path, I will make a beeping sound. They then have to leave the maze by the same route they came in and the next person makes an attempt. *Seems simple enough*, they think. Until I throw in a few wrinkles.

I tell them that everyone must get through the maze in under 15 minutes and they must complete the entire exercise without talking. Also, each team has an imaginary $1 million to spend. Every time there is a beep or a person talks, their team loses $1,000. And if they want a time-out, they have to pay $10,000. I then give the teams time to make a plan before I start the clock. Almost immediately, conflict arises among team members about how to keep the other team from learning what is happening on "our" team and how to avoid losing money. Participants go out of their way to avoid taking a time-out because they want to keep the money. And they do all manner of crazy things to keep the other side from seeing what their side is up to.

The result? I have never had a group complete the exercise successfully. This is because the money and the assumption that the activity is a competition distract the groups from achieving the goal. The sole objective of the exercise is to get *all* of the participants through the maze. There is no benefit to keeping any or all of the money. There are also no bonus points for completing the maze ahead of the other team. Both the money and the sense of competition draw the teams away from achieving their goal. They could watch each other carefully, use time-outs strategically and share information by talking.

It's a lesson in the important role that focus plays in success. Organizations and leadership teams tend to get drawn into minor diversions that keep them from successfully collaborating. Individuals face a similar problem when they spend a disproportionate amount of time on activities that are not important and neglect those that have a significant impact on their success. Just about anything can be a distraction. Sometimes people are distracted by money. Sometimes they are distracted by new relationships. Regardless of the source, anything that shifts focus away from the goal can be a problem.

The Hawthorne Effect

The effect of increased focus was the subject of a famous series of experiments in the late 1920s and early '30s at a Western Electric factory in the Chicago suburb of Hawthorne. The goal of the research was to explore the relationship between a worker's physical surroundings and their level of productivity. The experimenters separated workers into two areas and then began changing the working conditions of one of the groups to assess the effect. They first experimented with boosting the level of lighting. With each incremental increase, there was a significant increase in the workers' productivity. Then they tried other changes, such as altering the number of rest breaks or work hours, and there were additional increases in productivity. But it was when they started to reverse some of the changes that they found something really interesting. When they decreased the lighting and rest time, the workers continued to produce at the higher levels of efficiency. How could that be?

The increase in productivity came from the workers *thinking* about their performance rather than the changes being made in their work environment. When the researchers came into their environment and experimented with some adjustments, it was the first time the workers had been involved in assessing the factors affecting their efficiency. They worked more effectively because they were focused on their own productivity. We improve what we focus on improving.

The Skill of Focus

"Concentrate all your thoughts upon the work at hand. The sun's rays do not burn until brought to a focus."
ALEXANDER GRAHAM BELL

When I was coaching at Graceland, I had a young Mexican player named Isaias Diaz on the team. He was a decent player but not as good as he could be. In fact, at times, he had an upside-down spoon on his foot. But he had an incredible capacity to control his focus, such as when our team traveled to Brownsville, Texas, for a game, and we encountered a racist crowd. The fans stood right at the home team's sideline and yelled racist slurs at my Latino players. As the game progressed, it was clear that my right fullback was having trouble concentrating on the game. The crowd was succeeding at what they had in mind: they were getting

“Lack of direction, not lack of time, is the problem. We all have twenty-four-hour days.”

ZIG ZIGLAR

him off his game. So Isaias, who was on my side of the field, said, "Give it to me, Coach," and we swapped the fullbacks. Throughout the entire first half, Isaias played with only one focus—the game. He didn't even hear the crowd. And when we switched ends at the half, he went back to his side so that he was still right next to the hateful crowd. His focus did not extend past what he needed to do on the field, and so he was able to succeed.

In sport, there are generally two categories of focus: broad versus narrow, and inner versus outer. The first category, broad versus narrow focus, is the difference between a quarterback who needs to see the whole field and a golfer who has to concentrate exclusively on a single target. The second category, inner versus outer focus, is the difference between knowing what is happening inside you (heart rate, blood pressure, nervousness) and what is happening around you (what other people are doing, the weather, the ambient noise). The idea is that, depending on the situation, the athlete needs to develop and apply the appropriate kind of focus. Knowing this changes the way a coach sets up drills in practice and the way skills are developed for game-day execution.

In ordinary life, you shift focus all the time, but if you don't know it or aren't able to see what kind of focus is needed for a particular role or task, it's easy to zoom in on the wrong thing. Learning how to focus and how to determine what kind of focus is needed will help you improve—especially if you allocate time effectively to the tasks and activities that get you where you want to go. And once you learn how to control your focus, your belief in your ability to accomplish the task at hand grows.

Focus Builder #1: Focus on What You Want

Have you ever been in a situation where a noise is bothering you and, no matter what you do, you can't stop hearing it? Someone chewing gum on the train or tapping their pen in a meeting? This happened to health coach Daniel Cox, when he lived in an apartment on the main floor of a house. For weeks he obsessed about the noise from the family living above him: loud voices, stomping feet, music playing, chairs dragging. He grew so irate about it that he complained on his Facebook page. Some of his friends saw it and told him that the problem was with him and that he just needed to stop focusing on the noise. He took the feedback to heart and decided to get on with his life and try to ignore the racket. He lived the quiet life for weeks, which made him wonder what his neighbors had done to dampen the sound. Of course, the noise hadn't decreased at all—he had just stopped focusing on it.

Cox's conclusion from the experience was that you get what you focus on, so you ought to focus on what you want. It's a simple idea, but one that can be hard to establish in our daily habits: maintain focus on what you actually want to achieve. It is very easy to concentrate on trivial things that

WHAT YOU FOCUS ON IS WHAT YOU GET.

you don't actually care about. But no one can control your focus but you. What are you thinking about all the time? How are you spending your energy? What do you spend your time talking about? It's all up to you.

➤ WRITING PROMPT

List three issues that you spend time focused on even though they have very little to do with helping you achieve your goals:

1 ______

2 ______

3 ______

Now make a decision to stop paying attention to these issues and spend more time on what matters.

Focus Builder #2: Practice What Matters

Excellence is never an accident. It comes as a result of knowing exactly what you are trying to accomplish and preparing for that particular thing. If you go through life with only a vague notion of the skills, actions and ideas you need in order to perform particular tasks or succeed in certain settings, you will never be your best. For example, during the season when my team won the national championship, we knew we weren't going to be able to score goals the traditional way because our team's strength was not offensive skill. We had to do something differently. So I appointed two specialist players who stayed after practice three times a week to work exclusively on free kicks. We worked on them all season long, and when we got to the championship, every goal we scored came from a free kick instead of during the flow of play. We focused on building those skills, and it paid off.

FAMOUS FAILURE

Sidney Poitier went to his first audition and the casting director said, "Why don't you stop wasting people's time and go out and become a dishwasher or something?"

A more famous example is Abby Wambach, the most prolific scorer in the history of international soccer. With 184 goals, she has scored more than any other player—man or woman. And she scored one of the most exciting goals in the history of soccer during a quarterfinal match against Brazil in the 2011 World Cup. At the end of regulation time, the score was tied. Then, 28 minutes into a 30-minute extra time period, Brazil scored to take the lead 2–1. With the clock winding down, the Americans started to press, desperately trying to even the score. With only a bit of injury time left, a player named Megan Rapinoe crossed the ball in front of the Brazilian net and Wambach dove forward and headed it into the net. The game then went to penalty kicks and the Americans won. The play was so spectacular that it was selected by ESPN as the ESPY Best Play of the Year.

Soon after the game, I saw an interview with Wambach during which she was asked about the goal. She said simply, "I have been preparing for that goal my entire life." Right. It wasn't luck and it wasn't a fluke. She was known for her expertise at heading the ball. She had worked at it and worked at it, narrowly focused on that particular skill, until she could perform it effortlessly, even with the hopes of an entire country riding on her back.

Wambach's story is a model for all of us. When you practice, what is it you are trying to improve? If you are sloppy or unclear, you won't improve. Decide what you are working on and make a plan for how you will improve it. Then put in the time. It's about focusing on the precise skills you want to develop.

Focus Builder #3: Get the Resources You Need

When I first arrived at Ryerson, one of the areas that I just couldn't fix was our summer day camp program. I oversaw the athletics and recreation program in the heart of Canada's biggest city, with thousands of families needing affordable summer enrichment and childcare, and I could not get the program to make money. We even lost money during the summer when the city workers were on strike and there were

“Whenever you want to achieve something, keep your eyes open, concentrate and make sure you know exactly what it is you want. No one can hit their target with their eyes closed.”

PAULO COELHO

no programs available through Parks and Recreation. Why? Because the guy I had running the program was actually my intramural coordinator—camps were just a thing he did on the side.

After a few years of trying to get the program going without any success, I looked for an actual camp person to come in and do nothing but run the program. It took some work, but I eventually found a highly qualified camp director to take it on. As you would expect, the program was an immediate success, running a profit in the very first year and going on to become one of our most vibrant non-athletic revenue streams. All because I focused on providing the resources required for that particular program.

Focus Builder #4: Choose Your Own Definition of Success

I'm not the typical type-A personality leader. I don't use file folders. I often don't know where my wallet is. But all my life, I've had a passion for inspiring people to achieve big goals and I've had a desire to make a difference. At the beginning of my career, this desire created stress for me when I looked around at other leaders and saw that I wasn't like them. University presidents, deans and managers were high-achieving folk who were not (at least to my eye) like me. I focused too much on my deficiencies. I focused on what I was not. And it had a significant effect on my confidence. I began to believe the negative feedback I was getting from people who projected onto me their views about details and rules. We all have warts. Mine include not getting stuff turned in on time, or not saving a file the right way in the shared drive, or not filling out a form properly. A lot of "nots."

In time, and with exposure to some inspiring and very different leaders, I came to see that leadership is not a train on a track headed in the same direction for everyone. For me, leadership is about inspiring people to think about what they previously considered impossible. This may not be what leadership is to you. Different kinds of people can be and are leaders. I just needed to figure out what kind I was and get on with being my best version of it. Sure, I occasionally need to focus on my weaknesses and make a plan to compensate for them (like hiring people who can complement my skills), but figuring out my leadership style began with focusing on what I *had* and not on what I didn't have.

Focusing on my strengths allowed me to excel. I started to amplify the skills I had that were not widely available in the organizations I worked in. It made all the difference. I stopped looking for approval from others whose view of leadership, while valid and right for them, didn't apply to me. I started to focus on speaking, leading, coaching, building and rebuilding, and believing that these contributions are of great importance to organizations. As I lived by my own definition of success, my confidence grew and I was released from self-doubt, self-criticism and feelings that I would never be good enough. I was able to soar.

BE CAREFUL WHO YOU GIVE YOUR POWER TO... **DON'T LET OTHERS DISSUADE YOU FROM YOUR GOAL.**

CHAPTER 7 RECAP

The Skill of Focus

Focus Builder #1: Focus on What You Want

Develop your ability to ignore distractions and they will fall away if you focus on your goal.

Focus Builder #2: Practice What Matters

Practicing only takes you to the next level if you know exactly what you are trying to improve.

Focus Builder #3: Get the Resources You Need

Ensure that you are allocating time, energy and money to the goals you want to achieve.

Focus Builder #4: Choose Your Own Definition of Success

There are many versions of excellence—don't let other people define success for you.

8

FIND YOUR WHY

DISCOVERING YOUR TRANSCENDENT PURPOSE

"Your purpose in life is to find your purpose and give your whole heart and soul to it."

GAUTAMA BUDDHA

YOU ARE NOW equipped with an understanding of the five mental skills that combine to create self-confidence: positive thought, team building, grit, higher expectations and focus. Regardless of whether you already had some of these skills before you read this book, you now have a framework for developing them going forward. But before I wrap things up, I want to spend a bit of time talking about purpose.

If you think back to the famous innovators, leaders and adventurers highlighted in the Apple ad I talked about at the beginning of the book, these are people who exhibit the five mental skills of self-confidence. They are also people who were driven by a deep and abiding passion for something. They had a strong sense of who they were and why they were here. Their purpose was the animating force in their lives. To me, the five mental skills of self-confidence combined to create an amazing vessel, but it was purpose that put each of those people at the helm with a burning desire to get somewhere.

My own thinking about purpose started to take shape during my senior year as an undergraduate when I had a moment that felt like a sign from some higher power. At the time, I was madly studying for the MCAT so I could get into medical school. And though I didn't know it, I had a nagging sensation that this great big glorious dream of becoming a doctor and making my parents proud was somehow way off the mark.

One afternoon, I arrived in Professor Barbara Mesle's English class expecting the typical lecture and class discussion, when she digressed from the topic into a parable about meaning and purpose. I remember the details of the story only vaguely, but what I clearly recall was the moral: find work that you would volunteer to do and you will always be happy. That blew my mind. At the end of the class, I went straight to Polly and told her that I didn't want to be a doctor. So what *did* I want to do? I asked myself what I would volunteer to do. I had spent all of my high school and university years around sport: playing, supporting and coaching. I loved soccer more than anything. I loved being with people, building relationships and helping them improve themselves. It was that simple.

FAMOUS FAILURE

Oprah Winfrey was demoted from her job on the six o'clock news at Baltimore's WJZ-TV because she was getting too emotionally invested in her stories.

With this realization in mind, I applied to be a hall director in residence. It was the best decision I ever made.

Working in Gunsolley Hall, I got paid to invest in relationships. It didn't feel like working at all. Through that job, I met Dean of Students Tom Powell, who taught me that leadership is about investing and believing in people so they feel empowered. I also joined the soccer team as an assistant coach. Talk about meaningful. Everything I did, said and felt became about soccer. All I could think about was how to inspire my players to grow and improve. I was a 24-7 coaching machine. If they hadn't paid me, I wouldn't even have cared. It was amazing.

From those two early jobs, I was able to find my purpose in life: to be a creator of value. I want to invest in people and help them grow and achieve their dreams, leaving them better than they were before I came along. Happier. More confident. Stronger. Everything I have done—including writing this book—is an extension of that trajectory in my life. For me, coaching was never about winning, because if you take care of the way your players feel about themselves and each other, the winning will take care of itself. Sure, I had to develop the technical skills to coach well. I went to every coaching clinic, license course and workshop I could. I read every book and watched every video I could lay my hands on. I sought out any coaching mentor who would give me a moment of their time. I learned like crazy. I had to, because I wanted to be great at it. But the technical side of the game wasn't why I did it. I did it because I wanted to empower young people to dream big and find their path. I am an educator first and foremost.

Transcendent Purpose

"Don't aim at success—the more you aim at it and make it a target, the more you are going to miss it. For success, like happiness, cannot be pursued; it must ensue, and it only does so as the unintended side effect of one's dedication to a cause greater than oneself." VIKTOR FRANKL

I've coached two different university teams to a number-one national ranking, but soccer is simply a medium through which I perform my art. I am an educator who teaches personal qualities: believe in yourself; add value to your teammates; leave the world better than you found it; accept that hard work and dedication produce opportunities but not automatic success; and never be happy with good enough. I want everyone I work with to have confidence in themselves. That's why I do what I do. It's also why I have always loved working with student-athletes. Only a small number of them will ever play professionally. Most of them will have a life and a job like everyone else, which is why they need to know who they are and how to succeed. My purpose is my North Star—it guides me in everything I do. It is there for me when I face difficult decisions and don't know how to proceed. My purpose is also the source of the energy that inspires me every single day.

Periods of aimlessness or apathy plague all of us. Sometimes we lack direction. Sometimes we can't find our reasons for doing things. The way out is to go back to Professor

PURSUE YOUR PASSION AND SUCCESS WILL FIND YOU.

Mesle's question: What would you volunteer to do? Whatever the answer, that's the reason you are alive. I'm not talking about *what* you do—that's a side effect. I'm talking about *why* you do it. This is what best-selling author Daniel Pink calls "transcendent purpose"—a connection to some meaning greater than ourselves. Pink believes it's something that is present in all exceptional enterprises and that is far more motivational than money. I think he's right. It's why I always say to my players, "You'll never, ever remember your second goal, your third goal, what your fifth win was, but you'll always remember being part of a team that is committed to a culture of excellence."

Transcendent purpose can be genuinely difficult to find. You have to really know who you are and avoid being distracted or disoriented by what others think you should be. To assist you with developing a sense of your purpose and to help you make the most of what's contained in this book, here are three simple suggestions about how to find your purpose.

Purpose Finder #1: Forget about the Money

Daniel Pink makes a convincing case that the profit motive is nowhere near as powerful as the purpose motive. What he means is that we are not motivated by money to do great things. Our purpose isn't connected to our paycheck. Pink has learned through his research that three factors lead to better work performance and greater satisfaction in life:

autonomy, mastery and purpose. Being autonomous means being self-directed and trusted to do our work without being micromanaged. While we humans are social beings, we are more motivated by our inner drive than by external pressure. Mastery is achievement that follows a lengthy and gradual progression. It's that charge you feel when you can finally play the saxophone with pizzazz or paint the corners with your fastball. And purpose, as we know, is a sense of being connected to a cause greater than ourselves. Pink identifies purpose as the greatest motivator in our lives because it's the one that goes deepest.

Why are these three motivations so much more powerful than money? Because they all come from within us. They are all what researchers call intrinsic motivations—achieving them is the reward itself. We feel strong, capable and confident when we direct our own lives, master a skill and live with purpose. And money just can't do that. No matter how much of it you want or dream of having, money is by definition an extrinsic reward, like praise and fame. It won't build your confidence. And it can't be your transcendent purpose because it's something other people give you (or don't give you). It comes from the outside, and that's not where purpose comes from. Purpose comes from the heart and the guts. And people who live to chase the buck, confusing purpose with wealth, do not achieve the deep satisfaction of being connected to a greater cause.

And here's more good news (because if you ask me, it's a good thing that paychecks don't give us purpose): a 2010

"Your destiny is to fulfill those things upon which you focus most intently. So choose to keep your focus on that which is truly magnificent, beautiful, uplifting and joyful. Your life is always moving toward something."

RALPH MARSTON

Princeton study revealed that 85 percent of Americans, regardless of their annual income, felt happy each day. That's a whopping majority! In addition, the researchers found that emotional well-being tops out at an annual income of $75,000, which is about $83,000 in 2016. That's a decent paycheck and well above the US median, but it's not exactly "my puppy wears a diamond-studded collar" wealth. This suggests that if by some crazy stroke of luck you won millions in the lottery, you would feel no happier than if you earned $83,000, though you could sip your favorite beer from a gold chalice. So not only will money not provide you with a driving purpose, it won't even make you very happy. And chasing after it will only be an obstacle to living the life you seek.

Purpose Finder #2: Start with Why

When you go to figure out what your purpose is, make sure you don't get hung up on what you do as opposed to why you do it. That's the premise behind Simon Sinek's best-selling book *Start with Why: How Great Leaders Inspire Everyone to Take Action*. You may have seen Sinek's TED Talk and remember the image he draws of a series of concentric circles resembling a target. Using a company as an example, he explains that the outside circle is *what* a company does, the middle circle in is *how* they do it and the center is *why* they do it. Sinek's research illustrates that companies that begin with a clear emphasis on why they do what they do are far more successful than those that don't. They also have the happiest employees.

Most of us only have a vague sense of why we do what we do because we have never really made an attempt to express it. It can take years to know yourself well enough to articulate why you do what you do. And you might find that as you go through life, your "why" shifts or the words you use to describe it change. It doesn't matter. Sit down and write out a purpose statement that clearly expresses *why* you do what you do, not what you do or how you do it—whether you are doing it for yourself or for your organization.

➤ WRITING PROMPT

Think about your work and ask yourself why you do what you do. Now write out a draft purpose statement here:

"It is not enough to be busy; so are the ants. The question is: What are we busy about?"

HENRY DAVID THOREAU

Organizations are known for having mission and vision statements that aren't really expressions of why they do what they do. I once did some work for Cargill, the largest privately held company in the world that is primarily into food processing. When I was preparing to speak to a group of their employees, I tracked down the company's mission statement. It went like this: "Cargill provides food, agriculture, financial and industrial products and services to the world. Together with farmers, customers, governments and communities, we help people thrive by applying our insights and 150 years of experience. We have 155,000 employees in 68 countries who are committed to feeding the world in a responsible way, reducing environmental impact and improving the communities where we live and work." Hardly language that would make any employee jump out of bed in the morning. But then I found this: "Our purpose is to be the global leader in nourishing people." Wow.

It's the same for every individual. Phrases like "I am an excellent landscape designer" or "I practice law" or "I am a loving parent" are *what* statements. That's not your transcendent purpose. When you start writing your purpose down, stay away from what you do. Also, avoid *how* statements: how you do what you do, such as "I listen carefully to my clients" or "I study hard and work long hours" or "I pay attention to what my children need." Focus on expressing the *why*. What is it you believe? What kind of world do you want? What is the reason you are on this earth? What do you dream of accomplishing? Maybe just start with a list.

Look back on your life and see the trends. Ask other people what they think motivates you. Then sit down and make a statement about your *why*. You might end up with phrases like "Creating beauty in the world brings others joy" or "I believe in protecting people's rights and fighting injustice" or "I want my children to become confident and caring adults." Once you have your phrase, it will always be with you as a guide.

Purpose Finder #3: Choose Work that Suits Your Talents

There is nothing worse than shoehorning yourself into a job or a life that isn't you. It just won't work. So whether you read Tom Rath's *StrengthsFinder 2.0* or take the Myers-Briggs personality test or look at what you have done so far or ask a friend what they think you are good at, you need to figure out what tasks fit your talent and fulfill your purpose.

In my life, a good example of this came when I was a director at Gunsolley Hall. My partner in running the residence was a highly capable woman who was very different from me. I was creative, fluid, constantly engaged with lots of people and often clueless about what time it was or that there was even a thing called time. She was detailed, organized, budget-conscious and needed a push to smile and let loose. She was a wonderful, careful, conscientious person. I loved working with her, and we had a lot of fun. But when

"Without knowing what I am and why I am here, life is impossible."

LEO TOLSTOY

I started the job, it was upside-down world. I was assigned to do the scheduling and the budgets and she was responsible for the training and presentations to students. For the first little while, we muddled through it all, but stress levels started to increase as her sessions fell flat and I regularly messed up the details.

After thinking about it for a while, I eventually got up the gumption to suggest to her that we consider flipping our jobs. Her face lit up at the idea. I took over the people and presentation stuff and she got down and dirty with the details. *Pow!* It was the change we both needed. She was happy. I was happy. Our work was more alive and enjoyable. And, most of all, the residence ran better and we created a better experience for the students.

Knowing what you are good at—and finding your place so you can do your thing and be surrounded by others who complement what you offer—is key to finding your purpose and living and working with confidence. Don't worry about what you're supposed to be good at or fixate on talents you have that don't fill you with energy. Maybe you're a spectacular insurance adjuster, really top-notch at your job, but that gift doesn't make your heart sing. Maybe you feel most yourself on the weekends, working on your car and fixing your neighbors' various machines and devices. Maybe you're a mechanical genius and *that's* the talent that fills you with purpose. In which case, you may want to do something like that full-time. Finding a way to use the talent you most enjoy is part of a well-lived life.

Somewhere underneath your interest in developing self-confidence is your transcendent purpose. Articulating that purpose for yourself is one of the most powerful and inspirational things you can do to motivate your continual growth and energize your life. Finding your *why* doesn't have to be overly complicated, but it does require that you make the effort to have an authentic conversation with yourself about who you are and why you are here. The answer to those questions might shift and change as your life evolves, but if you can arrive at each stage of your growth with a clear sense of purpose, you will find that everything, including your belief in yourself, will come easier.

CHAPTER 8 RECAP

Discovering Transcendent Purpose

Purpose Finder #1: Forget about the Money
Design your life around autonomy, mastery and purpose instead of how much you earn and spend.

Purpose Finder #2: Start with Why
Figure out who you are, what you believe in and why you do what you do—not just what you do and how you do it.

Purpose Finder #3: Choose Work that Suits Your Talents
Find the perfect match between what you are good at and what you love to do.

9

ONE STEP AT A TIME

THE DAILY JOURNEY TO SELF-CONFIDENCE

"If we all did the things we are really capable of doing, we would literally astound ourselves."

THOMAS EDISON

WHEN I STARTED speaking about self-confidence, I had no idea how much the message would resonate with others. From the millions who have viewed my TEDx Talk to the thousands who have sat in the audience at my speeches, people have enthusiastically and warm-heartedly embraced the message. They have also reached out to me from all over the world. Here are a few examples:

The assistant director of a university career and internship center in the United States: "As an individual who has struggled with the concept of self-confidence but yet works to instill it in the students I work with every day, I found your message very poignant."

A professional struggling to restart her life after a major setback: "I have spent the last four years rebuilding myself into a new career after I had such a difficult time in my life that I had become homeless after a 22-year career. I heard your video for the first time almost a year ago and, even though my fears of losing my job are still there, they take a back burner to my belief in myself now."

A Ryerson student: "I still watch your TEDx lecture on self-confidence almost every day to remind myself that through repetition, persistence and self-belief, anything is possible. Your speech has inspired and motivated me to do better. Growing up through many struggles in my life, self-confidence was something I lacked, so your speech was truly inspiring and life-changing."

A life coach in Texas who works with young adults who are on the autism spectrum: "Your talk helped several young women with autism down here and also me personally. After your talk, I helped a group of them list different attributes about themselves, and they began to see that they were already practicing self-confidence. I asked them what would happen if we all really believed we had the qualities that were listed on the board, and one of them replied, 'The world would rock!'"

A member of the coaching staff of a Major League Baseball organization: "I appreciate your honesty in presenting your practice of self-confidence, and I am going to utilize your method by writing a letter to myself to express my self-worth and identify that I am capable of doing anything."

A woman in Portland, Oregon, starting a career as a writer: "I went from feeling mocked to full confidence. I wanted to thank you for making this misfit rebel feel like she is on the right path even though the chance is small."

An accounts manager for a manufacturing company in Pakistan: "As a former fat kid who was never good at sports (or anything as a kid), I have struggled with self-esteem and confidence issues all my life. Your talk was really inspiring. I hope your message can be heard by many more individuals."

The director of communications and marketing at a college in Georgia: "I have two children, a daughter who is 14 and a son who is 11, and my husband and I recently watched your TEDx Talk about self-confidence with them. The stories and lessons you shared connected with all four of us. We found ourselves laughing and nodding our heads, and it started a discussion about practice, believing in yourself, working to overcome challenges and realizing that failure isn't the end of the world. Your talk allowed our two kids to hear a message that we often share but isn't always heard because it's easy to ignore your own parents. They listened to you and then they talked to us."

AS YOU FINISH reading this book, remember that most self-confident people feel hesitant, worried and unsure at times. Lots of folks spend most of their time in a good mental and emotional space where they feel like they can climb a mountain or slay a giant, but they also have moments of self-doubt. Whenever you are in an unfamiliar situation, it's only natural for fear of failure to creep into your thoughts, especially if you are trying to elevate your performance to the next level or take on a bigger challenge. When that happens, follow the real-life, tangible steps outlined in this book to reduce your fear and doubt.

Self-confidence is not magic or voodoo. You've got to get out there and put in the sweat. You need to commit the hours, days, months and years of repetition and persistence that will develop your belief in your ability to accomplish the task at hand. Whether you're trying to kick a soccer ball, deliver a speech or lead a department, you'll have to risk making mistakes in order to grow. Self-confidence is not a skill that eliminates failure from your life. Quite the opposite. The more confident you are, the more often you will fail because confident people take risks.

Your ability to believe in yourself will lead you to the greatness you desire, but life will inevitably throw something your way that will yet again challenge your self-confidence. When those difficulties arise, come back to these pages and remind yourself of the mental skills of self-confidence. Until then, take the ideas of this book and go out to inspire confidence in those who matter to you, especially your children and the people you lead.

You got this.

ACKNOWLEDGMENTS

I OWE A DEBT of gratitude to the two institutions at which I have spent my entire career: Graceland University and Ryerson University. These organizations allowed me the freedom and autonomy to grow and learn, and provided me with opportunities that any young professional can only hope for. Thank you to all of the current and former players and teams I have coached and worked with. Everything that I know about human performance has emerged out of the living laboratory that you allowed me to create. Your willingness to follow me anywhere—even when I was mired in foolishness—made all the difference. We have done great things together, and I value the relationships we have built more than you can know. Also, my eternal thanks to my mentor, Tom Powell. We are all shaped immeasurably by our beginnings, and starting my career in Tom's "ministry of presence" made everything I have accomplished since then possible. Thanks also to Jesse Finkelstein, Trena White and the team at Page Two Strategies for shepherding this book into print. And thanks to my editors, Sumner & Lang, for being there with me every step of the way to help bring my vision for this book to life.

IVAN'S RECOMMENDED BOOKS

Top Six Must-Reads

My copies of these six books are well loved and dog-eared. I think of them as books that set me on my path.

Bach, Richard. *Jonathan Livingston Seagull*. New York: Scribner, 2006.

Jackson, Phil. *Sacred Hoops*. New York: Hyperion, 2006.

Jenner, Bruce. *Finding the Champion Within*. New York: Simon & Schuster, 1997.

Millman, Dan. *Way of the Peaceful Warrior*. New York: New World Library, 2000.

Robbins, Tony. *Awaken the Giant Within*. New York: Free Press, 2003.

Wooden, John. *They Call Me Coach*. New York: McGraw Hill, 2004.

Other Reference Reads

These six books provided important ideas that I have used during my career.

Achor, Shawn. *The Happiness Advantage*. New York: Crown Business, 2010.

Bandura, Albert. *Self-Efficacy: The Exercise of Control*. New York: W.H. Freeman, 1997.

DiCicco, Tony, and Colleen Hacker. *Catch Them Being Good: Everything You Need to Know to Successfully Coach Girls*. New York: Viking Penguin, 2006.

Duckworth, Angela. *Grit*. New York: Scribner, 2016.

Dweck, Carol. *Mindset: The New Psychology of Success*. New York: Ballantine Books, 2016.

Pink, Daniel. *Drive*. New York: Riverhead Books, 2011.

Sinek, Simon. *Start with Why: How Great Leaders Inspire Everyone to Take Action*. New York: Portfolio, 2009.

LOOKING FOR MORE?

You can follow Ivan on Twitter: @DrIvanJoseph

To hire Ivan as a speaker:

In Canada: www.speakers.ca/speakers/dr-ivan-joseph/
In the United States: www.nationalspeakers.com/speakers/speaker_details.php?id=672

ABOUT DR. IVAN JOSEPH

IVAN JOSEPH, PHD, leads individuals, teams and organizations to success. While serving as a professor and soccer coach at Graceland University (a century-old liberal arts university in southern Iowa), Dr. Joseph developed the soccer program from the ground up, leading both the men's and women's teams to a number-one national ranking and the men's team to a national championship—in just five years.

The National Association of Intercollegiate Athletics recognized Dr. Joseph as National Coach of the Year in 2006, and three times he received Coach of the Year recognition in the Heart of America Athletic Conference.

In his current role as Director of Athletics at Ryerson University in Toronto, Ontario, Dr. Joseph is guiding the transformation of the Ryerson Rams athletic department, improving team performance while at the same time raising the academic average of athletes.

In addition to coaching and teaching, Dr. Joseph spearheaded the creation of a premier multi-field soccer complex at Graceland. He raised significant private and public funds to

build the facility, endow scholarships, enhance programs and organize international matches for his teams in Brazil, Canada and Europe. In addition, the $100-million renovation of historic Maple Leaf Gardens at Ryerson University was recently completed under Joseph's leadership.

An educator and organizational leader who has brought about cultural transformation, Dr. Joseph is a sought-after speaker on developing personal and organizational leadership. He talks about self-confidence, the "grit" to persevere in spite of setbacks and leading teams to success. Dynamic and inspiring, the stories and lessons he shares apply to business and to life.

Born in Guyana, Dr. Joseph grew up in Toronto, where he was a nationally ranked high school track-and-field athlete. He was recruited to Graceland as a student-athlete in 1993.

Ivan Joseph has a BA in Physical Education and Health from Graceland, a MS in Higher Education Administration from Drake University and a PhD in Sports Psychology from Capella University.

CPSIA information can be obtained
at www.ICGtesting.com
Printed in the USA
FFHW02n0555061018
48714537-52764FF

9 780995 830004